To Janet & Harold,
Happy Christmas
2005

Hans, Lorna + Eric

Daily Reflections
2005

Daily Reflections
2005

Foreword

In the age of frenzied lifestyles and hectic schedules, most of us have precious little time to gather our thoughts or contemplate our emotional susceptibilities. It is recognised however that the simple act of expressing and sharing our thoughts and experiences with others can very often provide us with that much-needed release.

With this in mind Triumph House have collaborated with the authors, combining their creative ingenuity with our skilful expertise to present you with a prestigious anthology you will want to cherish and treasure for years to come.

Daily Reflections 2005 is a beautifully crafted anthology of unequalled calibre. Bursting at the seams with first-rate examples of spiritually stimulating poetry and prose. An exclusive collection of intuitive and inspirational literary accomplishments, for every day of the coming year, providing an enjoyable read that will brighten and enrich the days of the reader time and time again.

Sharon Spencer
Editor

Contents

Daily Reflections

Daily Reflections
2005

Poems, Thoughts
& Reflections

My Biggest Mistake

I've made mistakes
(some so big they beggar belief)
but the biggest mistake I'll ever make
will be my last: when I finally give up
give in, and never try again.

Robert Black

Daily Reflections

Take every day as it comes,
Enjoy your life and have lots of fun.

Always keep on trying your best,
You're sure to pass life's test.

Spend your time with family and friends,
Absorbing the happiness it sends.

Have magical moments with memories to treasure.
It's these precious memories that'll give you most pleasure.

Keep in touch with your affections,
Remember this as part of your daily reflections.

Pam Sahota

I Remembered

I was having many troubles
Tears welled my eyes
Hardened to events
Immune to surprise

Head in hands
Searching for a way
Then came the prize
I remembered to pray

I told of my sorrows
Automatic somehow
My eyes were closed
My head a low bow

I let loose my fears
That shadowed the weeks
Salted tears
Tumbled my cheeks

Cried over past hurts
How I couldn't cope
How talking in prayer
Was my last hope

A gentle peace
Settled over me
Allowing my troubles
To leave gracefully

I was having many troubles
I'm glad of the day
I bowed my head
And remembered to pray

Angelia Burke

The Fiddle

My daddy played the fiddle at the fireside every night
He'd rosin up the bow and make sure all the strings were tight.
He'd then invite my sisters out to dance upon the floor.
The reels were fast, the jigs were class, the horn pipes, they were slower.

My daddy played the fiddle in the very early morn
I would follow him with buckets to fill the bag with corn
He'd then head off across the soil his arm going to and fro
To carefully sow the seeds the earth would finally grow

My daddy played two fiddles, each one had a unique sound
When he played the first one the neighbours gathered round
He'd fill our house with music and all would clap and fling,
The bow upon the strings would make the fiddle sing.

Now when he played the second one, you just could never tell,
For Daddy in his hay day could play them both so well,
And even in the early morn when no one stood around
The music played to cast the seed into its earthly ground.

Eugene Fullerton

The Snowdrop

The small green shoots begin to show
Through hardened ground and winter snow,
Oh what a lovely dress it wore, the dainty little snowdrop.
The sweetest dress of green and white,
To the eye a pure delight,
Heralding that spring's in sight, the dainty little snowdrop.
Then summer comes, the snowdrops cries,
The springtime whispers its goodbyes,
In the midst the snowdrop dies,
The dainty little snowdrop . . .

The summer comes and shines so bold,
But at length it feels the cold,
As autumn shines in red and gold, silent lies the snowdrop.
The autumn leaves are now all shed,
The yellow, red and gold are dead,
Now it's wintertime instead, sleeping is the snowdrop.
Be gone! Cold winter winds that blow,
We don't want you anymore -
The small green shoots begin to show,
The dainty little snowdrop.

Marian Theodora Maddison

God's Wide, Wide World

A child much loved - to kin and friends close-tied -
Nightly I knelt in prayer to share with God
The happiness and tears of every day.

I would promise to be good and pray that He would send
His special blessing on my family and friends . . .
And then (but only if He felt He had the time)
He might bestow a kindly blessing on -
The wide, wide, world out with my ken.

Childhood and rebellious youth flew past.
Life taught me much - and fast. War-torn our nights and days.
Facing the 'great unknown' - no family, no friends -
I stood alone.
Fear triggered need of prayer, to share once more
With God my inmost thoughts and reveal my faith was weak.

Amid the noise of guns - bombs - calling voices -
There came to me 'the still small voice of calm'
'Be not afraid; my created world I do not forsake
            I care for all.'
Home - family - friends - much I had lost
But found again my *God.*
Within His keeping I have soldiered on.

In age my daily prayers now ask a special blessing
On *all* who share *God's wide, wide world.*
He points us to the Cross - alive His promise
To guide us to eternity.

Christina Crowe

Colours Of Life

W ithhold not the purist thought
H ands that help are loved
I t's something that cannot be bought
T hese are the keywords of life
E mbrace - what Jesus taught.

R eturn to the ties that bind
E nrich your heart and mind
D eny injustice - be kind.

G reatness is wisdom gleaned
R ichness a state of mind
E nrich your soul and find
E nvy, greed - from your mind weaned
N ever let the sun go down - blind.

Y our faith is bright like sunrays
E ach happy moment a gift
L ive life, never let a rift
L ead you down - lift your gaze
O nward and upward, joy your goal
W ith love for fellow creatures in your soul.

B lazon only love throughout your life
L ove of beauty, truth, benevolence, cheer
U se faith to lighten another's load, wear
E ach waking moment a smile - deny strife.

B ecause we are born to die - live
L oving life - another's trespass forgive
A lways repay kindness with like
C leave to the teachings of Christ
K eep piety in your heart all your days.

Valerie Hall

Daily Reflections

Think Positive

Every morning when we wake up,
It's another new day.
We should be grateful,
Count our blessings,
Give God thanks for
Guiding,
Protecting,
And keeping us.
It's another chance to make changes,
Don't look back,
Or, think about
What should have been,
Could have been,
Would have been,
And might have been.
Instead,
We must look forward,
Focus on our dreams,
Think positive,
Be strong,
Believe in ourselves,
And live every minute of that day to the full,
Because no one knows
What tomorrow will bring.

Pauline E Reynolds

Born Under The Star Of Bethlehem

'No room at the inn,' the Holy Family was told,
Nowhere to go and they had to be bold.
The time was near for the birth of our Saviour,
No need to fear - for they held God's favour.

The Lord was born in a simple stable,
The Star of Bethlehem shined upon His cradle.
The power of the Almighty, God the Father, is with You to eternity,
Mankind's salvation born to the Virgin Mary for generations to see.

The Three Kings came, in adoration - with gifts,
Gold, frankincense and myrrh and fell to their feet.
They bowed before the Son of God, Jesus Christ -
In his Holy Mother's arms, to adore and greet.
The merciful King of Kings - God made Man
Born under the Star of Bethlehem.

The silence of the night was broken with song,
The angels came to announce that the
World's Merciful Salvation was born.
Gloria in Excelsis they sang in full voice,
Blessed is the heart that believes in God's choice.

Kinga Gray-Grzeczynska

Daily Reflections

Epiphany

(January 6th)

These whistling frosty nights,
bold stars above our heads,
we dream of eastern Magi, rich in knowing,
burdened with desire, earnestly seeking
truth.

Through icy teeth
the forest sharply draws its breath:
naïve, the scholars share their query with a king,
are partly duped and start a pilgrimage, their guide
a star.

Pagan shrines are all they know,
to science and discovery, not deity.
Thank God for curiosity, even more for dreams.
Thank God for early gentile faith. Thank God
for Love.

Louise Swanston

A Song

Where Your feet pass
The lame are healed
The blind can see
The dumb can talk
Where Your feet pass
The soul is healed
Come Jesus, come to all of us

Where Your feet pass
All sins forgiven
Where Your feet pass
Love does reign
Where Your feet pass
New life is given
And the Lazarus
All will rise again

Where Your voice is heard
There is no war
Where Your voice is heard
There are no poor
Where Your voice is heard
Only trust is there
Where Your voice is heard
There is no despair

Where Your feet pass
The deaf can hear again
Where Your feet pass
All quarrels cease
Where Your feet pass
Is found true forgiveness
Where Your feet pass
There is only peace.

Elizabeth Mary Caswell

Daily Reflections

First Communion

Yellow blooms
White blooms
Bright balls of sunshine
Sharing bread
Sharing wine

Resounding responses
Whispered responses
Voices in union
First prayers from my heart
First Communion

Finding God
Following God
We enter this day
Each lifting our cross;
Each stepping out on our way.

Nancy Black

I Live On Still

Life is not ours to say we own
'Tis but a lease, 'tis but a loan
And now this day to be repaid
Life's but a shadow on a shade

For what we were, stay overjoyed
For what we are can't be destroyed
Whilst in thy heart I am not gone
Another room, where I speak from

Think of the good times, not the sad
Remember the love that we once had
Yes I am here, death did not kill
Within thy being, I live on still.

Colin W Weston
(The Bamber Bridge Bard)

Daily Reflections

Faith And Hope

Let the Lord grant you strength and assurance in your life
To have faith to cope with the anxieties and strife
The peace of God which transcends all understanding and adulation
Will guard your hearts and minds from trepidation

Let the Lord give you trust, above all
Problems can't be changed by worrying, however big or small
Whether you worry or not, tomorrow will come
And each day has enough troubles of its own, for some

Let the Lord gently enter your heart and soul
To bestow inner peace, restore certitude, and console
Christ Jesus promised you hope, not despair or sorrow
Have faith and trust for the impending events of tomorrow.

Julia Keiser

Believe

Fragility in its utmost form,
Yearning souls so far apart.
Unyielding desire to be reborn
To settle in each other's hearts
Cling on to hope when all is lost
When faith is damned and evil winds
Hold those dreams despite the cost
For true love soars on angels' wings
Eternal hope may rise and fall
Still burns bright the flame with time
Never waning through it all
Maturing like the finest wine
Until the floodgates open wide
And in an instant life begins
Hearts are open step inside
And feel true love from deep within.

Joanne Firth

Dream World

As I discharged my grandad's duties
In the park the other day
I slipped to the realms of fantasy
As I watched the children play.
If the world was run by children,
Say to the age of ten,
What a wonderful place we'd live
In, no teens, no women, no men!
There would be no politicians
So there would be no wars.
Only love and understanding
And ever open doors.
Life would be just one big game
To be enjoyed by all.
Sympathy when things go wrong
Picked up when we fall.
Child's world knows no boundaries
They wait if they're behind,
No ethnic bias or prejudice
Cos they're all colour-blind.
Sadly this is a silly dream
Of a man in his later years
But also a man who much prefers
Laughter instead of tears.

Eric Calland

Winter's Day

A parrot comes to call each day
Has a feed then flies away
His visits show a brighter way
To wipe away the winter grey

Red and yellow, blue and green
The brightest bird I have ever seen
Bet he can be very mean
Local birds aren't too keen

They give the parrot loads of space
Despite the fact he's in their place
Discretion never was disgrace
Better than retreat in haste

This parrot isn't sense-wise bright
Not the usual winter sight
Should be in his cage at night
Or jungle-bound at treetop height

Instead he chooses here to stay
To sleep and eat and maybe play
For me, in times so very grey
I'm glad he comes to call each day

Ray Ryan

The Gift

Each day is a gift, let's live it
It's part of God's great plan
Open your eyes and look around you
See the beauty while you can.

The splendour of a rainbow
As it arches across the sky
The sunrise in the morning
Such loveliness we cry.

The snow that covers the ground
On a cold winter's day
The dewdrops on the roses
And the smell of new mown hay.

As we go on life's way
Let us be thankful for each day
As season follows season
Are we here for a reason?

Or do we take for granted
All these wondrous things?
We should say thank You Lord
Thank You Lord for everything.

Mary Rivers

Lost, For A Moment

I'm in a long dark tunnel Lord,
I seem to have lost my way.
Everything's just closing in,
It's difficult to pray.

It's not You who's abandoned me,
I've let go of Your hand.
Burdened by the cares of life,
I know You understand.

So, for the moment Lord
Please carry me along,
Lead me through this darkness
Until again I'm strong.

And even as I write these words,
A light begins to glow.
The peace returns back in my heart,
A love only You can show.

Thank You Lord for being there
Each and every day.
I know You are the potter
And I must be the clay.

Mould me as You will Lord,
Make me really strong
And as I walk with You Lord,
The dark tunnels will seem less long.

Gwendoline Jones

Time For Others

The happiness I seek is hard to find,
It may just be a state of mind,
But as I go from day to day,
I meet with sorrow along the way,
Some folk I see are at their end,
Without a hope, without a friend,
It's only then I tend to care,
And offer love for them to share.
My just reward is one of peace,
To know my love will never cease,
So as we go along life's way,
Share your love, make someone's day.

K Wathen

Get Well, Sweetheart

How sad a summer garden, in the cool and misty rain,
With scarce a leaf that flickers, or a pool with droplets' rings.
Stay quiet, and wait with patience for a bird that sweetly sings
A note to give us hope that summer's warmth will come again.

First leaves of autumn spiral down, and sprinkle gently, darkly brown.
Bright duckweed covers water, though the boatmen lie so still.
There's ne'er a goldfish to be seen, examine where you will.
Reflections once showed lilies, but they're dull in garden's frown.

Close your eyes, sweet Nature. Let the bats flit by and eat.
Relax into your slumber. Hazy dreams wipe through your mind.
Dream on about your garden. Golden roses you will find.
I'll hold your hand through darkest hours. At sunrise we shall meet.

The sun will catch the brilliant blooms. Fresh light comes to your eyes.
You're feeling strong. A bright new day flows free across your bed.
Sweet smelling flowers run clear inside the channels of your head.
Garden petals flood with warmth. Your breath will energise.

The fever's gone: the stiffness eases: strength takes time to build.
But soon you take my arm, sweet love, and I will guide you through
Where blooms you've planted reach out here
And share the sun with you.
Each breath is won, each step a triumph.
With dew my eyes have filled.

David Light

God's Showers Of Blessings

God sends His blessing from above
With His miraculous creation and wondrous love
Each little gift that He does prepare
With the beauty of nature, that we may share

To the brightness of the sun, during summertime
When each little bird, sings in rhyme
When blackbirds are heard, with their high-pitched voice
Waking up other birds, through their notes of rejoice

Especially through the earliest morn
As the thrush wakes up, giving a yawn
Until, the blackbird soon flies through the sky
Catching insects, as the swift passes by

While, the female protects her offspring in her nest
But, really she knows what is best
The magpie watches, with his scheming ways
Till, the blackbird flies back, quite wary of his prey

He watches the magpie, whilst perched on a tree
The swift, sits beside him, oh, feeling so free
A friend he becomes with the blackbird's charm
Listening to his high notes of alarm

The swift flies towards the magpie, with fast beating wings
The magpie's thieving games are over, it seems
He quickly then flies towards the woodland's trees
The winds then did hail, with a sharp sudden breeze

All is calm, with the sound of the blackbird's chatter
While other birds join in, with the thrush's flute natter
Till the day goes by, and twilight appears
Till, the nightingale's rich notes, sounds with notes of cheers

Showing their white beams across their throats
Through God's showers of blessings, with each bird's notes.

Jean McGovern

Daily Reflections

Daily the human race survives
And the plight of many brings tears to one's eyes
Ideally if the world was a better place
Laughter, no famine, a happy face
You and yours safe but that is not the case.

Realising this, makes life precious by far
Evening reflections, yes wish on a star
For many, wishing brings hope, not despair
Long suffering drug users, illness, not fair
Everyone deserves a chance, someone to care
Counting on the good times, they are there somewhere
Tomorrow a new day, hope in one's heart
In positive thinking, a new start
Onward and forward, a life for to live
Not for the faint-hearted, a hand to give
Supportive and helpful, ready to perceive and believe.

Sheila Macdonald

Daily Reflections

Opportunity

(Isa.25 1-9, 1 John 5. Songs of songs 2:1, Matt. 7.7)

Laid in a manger, hung on the cross
Jesus lives today to save the lost.
Risen victorious, o'er death and the tomb,
The 'Rose of Sharon', forever in bloom.

As rose petals hold cold raindrops,
And are dried by streaming sunrays,
So human sorrows are softened
By the enveloping touch of God's grace.

'Ask and it will be given.
Seek, and you will find.
Knock, and the door will be opened.'
He's waiting our needs to supply.

A R Harcus

Freedom

The Son is the image of the Father,
the radiance
of His glory and Majesty.

The Father's power and mighty strength
exerted in His Son
raised Him from the dead.

The Son is at the right hand of the Father,
our mediator,
giving us purification.

The Son's one sacrifice has made perfect
those being made holy,
today and tomorrow.

The Son is the same; yesterday,
today,
forever.

Through the Son, we may approach the Father
with confidence
and freedom.

Derek Norris

Daily Reflections

The Earth Is Mine

To sit alone
To watch the colours grow
To feel the silence
That others long to know

To touch the wind
And ride the light
To know the moon
And stars
That light the darkness
Of the night

To hold all Earth
For just a moment in time
To know all this
Is to know
The Earth is mine.

Janet Vessey

God's Perfect Plan

Looking at the day
Sunny and bright
At the freeness of the breeze
And the green of the trees
I see
Truth
God's perfect plan of life

Each branch and leaf
Birds sitting on boughs
All together
Giving each other
Space and time
Compromise

I feel they could easily see me
And like the bird in the gilded cage
Believe I am trapped
In a man-made prism of wood, stone and glass

Little do they know
That at last like the picture outside
Shaped in serenity
Having found
Truth
I just have to be brave
Take the hand of courage
And be proud to say 'God made me! and
I am part of this beautiful day'.

Paulette Martin

The Book Of Life

O, to be inscribed in the book of life,
By the creative hand of
The calligrapher Divine.
A regal document of
Eternal acceptance;
Majestically resting upon
The altar of the Most High;
Untouched by human hands.

Amidst the festive angelic gathering;
On the great day of the
Sacred book's opening;
Every indelible loving entry disclosed,
Will guarantee that soul
The crown of life.

Then, what anthems will resound
From the lips of the redeemed?
And what songs of gladness
Pervade the celestial atmosphere?
O, for that magnificent day;
Known only to His saints,
Whose names were found in
The Lamb's book of life.
The book, the book,
The great book of life.
Hallelujah.

Azariah Ephratah

Spirit Of Love

Spirit of love shine your light on me,
Fill me with love for eternity
Make me considerate, kind and sincere
Always understanding to those who are near.

Spirit of love with your golden rays,
Help me through the most troublesome days
When times are dark let your light shine through
Protect me in everything that I do.

Spirit of love with your powerful light
Shed your love on the world tonight.

Christine Hardemon

Prayers

*(To Andy for all your help and inspiration
Heather, always in my thoughts)*

May God answer your prayers.

The time that you are going through may seem so hard to bear
and that no matter what you do there are shadows everywhere.

Yet please try to remember that you have so much strength within
and if you call upon its power you'll see where you should begin
for this calm spot within you.

It's where Almighty God abides and He is there for you always.

For you to walk beside.

So love Him with all your heart and there'll be an answer
to your prayer.

Nancy Elliott

Inspiration

I don't know where these words come from
But I always know what to say
Like someone talking in my head
Guiding me every day

They always have the answers
But I don't always hear
That's when the problems start
And I get filled with fear

I have to learn to open my ears
To hear all they have to share
Think of the wonderful things I could learn
From my friends who always care

When I try really hard to communicate with them
All I get is a head full of blanks staring at the wall
It's when I'm not trying I hear their soft words
Then I know I'll be okay, they'll catch me if I fall

It's comforting to hear them
Helping me to get things right
I know I'm looked after
By my angel day and night.

Dana Pax Carpano

Walk In Zen

(A thought away)

Why frown when you can smile?
Why fear when you can have faith?
Why misery when there is joy?
Why have a bad thought when you can have a good one?
Why look down when you could look upwards, towards the stars?
Why fight when there can be compromise?
Why stop now when you are capable of so much more?
Why all this angst, when you could just accept 'what is'?
Why walk in darkness, when the light is just a thought away?

You are the reason why –
You have to want to do it,
You can make it happen.

Lynda Arnold

A Winter's Day

Tentative ears against the wind
The song of winter enters in
The day, as fresh as evergreen
Its endless seasonal whispering

The sky, in its reigning glory
Alight with colour merging wide and tall
With blues, indigos, reds and golds
The season's day, its story told

The air so sweet, so mint, so sweet
The respective aura of refreshment
And the pitter-patter of heavenly rain
Sent to tone down the greys of the brick pavement

A song, a song to add to beauty
The birds, angels to this wintry haven
Abide with the day's subtle starlit duty
Adorn and decorate with winter's making

Alas this serene picture is short to last
Will melt away to become the past
But come twelve months near new year's end
And winter's bloom will begin once again.

Mary Ibeh

I Saw A Rainbow Today

I saw a rainbow in the sky today,
It arched the fields to far away,
And the clouds on one side gloomed dark and low,
And big drops fell from the arc in the 'bow.

The far side was cloudless, and the sky was blue,
It was lighter and brighter for the sun shone through,
As if the day itself was split in two minds,
What weather to give, so gave us both kinds.

I could look at the sun and the rain together,
See a different beauty in each kind of weather.
We are so reliant on all things elemental,
And any imbalance would be detrimental.

There are always two ways to look at all things,
The good and the bad that all life brings,
If we can see purpose in the rain and beauty in the sun,
Then our understanding of life will have truly begun.

Kate Laity

Magic

There's magic in the rising moon.
In a flower whose petals close at noon.
Colour is magic wherever you look;
There's magic in a story book.

The wind which blows through the trees,
The white-topped waves on silvery seas.
Feathered friends flying swiftly by,
A picture reflected in human eye.

A windmill, a clock or a plane,
A beachball, a brick or a train.
A bus or tram, marmalade or jam,
A brass band or grain of sand.

Father and daughter, mother and son,
When two hearts now meet as one.
It's hard to match the magic of a smile
Or the face of wonder on a child!

L E Growney

Not Far Away

Overarching God,
Creator
Of this dazzling
Yet baffling universe,
Made approachable to us
Through the face of Jesus,
Whose short life
And savage death
Upturned this world,
And whose Spirit now
Enfolds us,
Can You comfort the ones
Who lost husband and daughter,
Who lost husband and son,
To assure them
Their loved ones
Are not far away?

You have promised
You are with us always,
No less now they have gone
To be with You.
Must that not mean
The closer that we live to You
The closer they are to us?

So may we live this 'in between time'
Until our day shall come
And we shall be once more
Entirely one.

Kathleen Davey

Entry Into Life

Regret and fear, excitement and ecstatic hope
All swirl around the human heart as changes loom,
Then swamp, then ebb into the distant memory
As future drowns the past and bears us on its crest.

Departure from the warmth and safety of the womb;
The rhythmic silence and the comfort of the dark
Are left behind and not by choice but with regret
As cold and noise and garish light bring fear and rage.

Excitement and ecstatic hope have had no part
In this departure so unsought, so rude, so quick;
But they will surely follow after as the joy
Of life renewed floods in to bathe the newly-born.

But what of death – unsought but not to be denied?
Departure from the shaky safety of this world
Need not be partnered by regret and rage and fear
But by excitement springing from ecstatic hope.

The prospect of such glory, entry into life
So full of joy and warmth, of light and laughing love,
Of boundless freedom to explore the mysteries
Of time and space, and beauties hitherto unknown –

Such prospect beckons with divine authority
For Christ has crossed and crossed again this line,
Departing from this world to bathe in life renewed.
We too can cross, while leaving rage and fear behind.

Vaughan Stone

The Candle And The Wire

(Words from deep in the soul)

You'll never know how I feel,
Even though you think you will.
Even though words inspire,
I can't see through the fire.

In my dreams I see
Things that frighten me,
But your words inspire,
Brought by the candle and the wire.

Help me, help me, I know you care.
Tell them, tell them, they know you're there.

Friends that I won't see,
Some are dead you see,
Although they heard the voice,
They longed to have a choice.

Though I am young, I'm old,
My body aches with cold,
Though my mind is tired,
I focus on the candle and the wire.

Help me, help me, I know you care.
Tell them, tell them, they know you're there.

Light will shine for some,
Freedom may well come,
Right to speak out loud.
Right to stand so proud.

In my dreams I see
A better place for me,
Let your words inspire,
Through the candle and the wire.

Help me, help me, I know you care.
Tell them, tell them, they know you're there.

John Cook

Cuckmere Haven

In the sun we walked together hand in hand
along the meanders of the River Cuckmere
to the pebbly beach that holds the sea at bay,
where seven sisters guard the channel
as they have done for centuries.

She gathered the swirl of her white petticoat
and, tucking it into her knickers,
went rushing into the icy water
giggling and shrieking like an eight year old.
Seven Sisters shining their white petticoats to the world
and the eighth sister for me.

I lay on the pebbles and soaked up the sun.
Then she joined me
and together we felt the surge of the tide
reverberating through the stones beneath us
like the beat of the earth's heart deep below.
I felt her diaphragm –
the beat was there too, but much faster.

She said this was a 'golden day';
one to keep in a box and remember for ever.
I agreed and said we'd have many more,
but I never saw her again.
She can put this in her box to remind her,
and, maybe, one day she'll return.

Tim Nice

Constant

The gates of love are open
Waiting for us to walk inside
To share our love together
And to wear it with pride.
Because my love for you is constant
Ever faithful, ever true
All my life it will so remain
As my heart belongs only to you.

Lady M

Your Cross Is My Command

I found the cross when it found me
a cross that streams serenity
a cross that bridges rivers of sin
a cross befitting a Christian King.

A cross that knights the tiniest soul
and shepherds them from Hell and holes
a cross confessed to every tongue
when knees are bent, every one.

A cross for blood of any colour
the cross commands we love each other
the cross commands o'er death and grave
the cross commands that we are saved.

Sean Kinsella

With Or Without

Without sentiment there is no value
With trepidation there can be no fear
Without deceit there is no truth
Without cause there can be no meaning.

With determination comes achievement
With hope the spirit thrives
With fewer words lives sincerity
With controversy lies competition.

Without dilemma there is no choice
Without admission there can be no guilt
Without difference there is no individuality
Without tears there can be no sympathy.

With variety breathes harmony
With encouragement brings result
With vigilance security is maintained
With prayer comes absolution.

Without sorrow there is no joy
Without regret there can be no forgiveness
Without confession there is no contrition
Without trophy there can be no champion.

With time patience is realised
With faith purpose can be attained
With support difficulties can be reduced
With humility friends are plentiful.

Without pigment there can be no colour
Without dictatorship there is no oppression
Without delivery there can be no promise
Without peace there can be no freedom.

Pauline Pickin

Untitled

(For my Paula)

There comes a point within our life
when sadness comes our way,
The strength we need to carry on
can sometimes slip away,
Such hurt and pain can drain our soul
cause sorrow in our heart,
Then slowly with each passing day
our world can fall apart,
You feel alone your voice unheard
the answers can't be found,
You look around for someone's hand
to lift you from the ground,
This pain you feel you're scared to share
your sanity on show,
Just why your life now feels this way
you daren't let people know,
Yet someone's there to help you through
upon this loving Earth,
To help you find the strength you need
and give you back your worth,
Your confidence in time will grow
bring back your self esteem,
The happiness you thought you'd lost
no longer seems a dream,
Express in words just how you feel
when sad and feeling low,
You'll find within these words revealed
the hurt will soon let go,
Soon you'll stand upon your feet
no longer on the floor,
This pain that forced you to the ground
you now have shown the door,
Believe in what you feel is right
the person who is you,

Don't let others put you down
or change your point of view,
So if you're stood upon the edge
that drops down into Hell,
Remember that you're not alone
we've all been there as well,
Just stop and take a look around
you'll find an angel near,
Someone who will understand
and lend a caring ear.

Rick Thorp

59

My Bird Stand

My dear husband made me a bird stand
And he has put it on the front lawn
What it is for the birds don't understand
They look at it so forlorn
The wood pigeons came first and couldn't get inside
They walked on the roof and round the side
So we took the roof off and whacko, starlings, sparrows came in
dozens and even a crow
Then they were fighting over crumbs
I thought by gum, I am glad they have found out what it is for
Or otherwise my husband would have been mighty sore
Now the birds know all about it
We are all happy no doubt about it
We put the roof back on
Then we watch all the fun.

May Ward

Fully Qualified Survivor

(Inspired by the River Ribble)

It is years since I saw a raindrop,
penetrate your crystal surface.
Sent a stone skimming merrily,
across your shimmering flanks.
Gazed languidly at the shifting hues,
beneath your smooth veneer.
Yet, you are still here.

Oh yes, you're a survivor alright,
imbued with a gritty resolve.
A big lad, in more ways than one.
Big enough to fight the frost,
when it makes your flow grow rigid.
Big enough to thwart the sun,
when it sucks your tongue bone dry.
Big enough to absorb rain,
when it hammers out a beating.
Yet still come back for more.

Oh yes, you're a tough one alright!
Accepting every challenge on those
broad and willing shoulders.
Never fighting shy of woe
and the cruel blows it strikes.
Not afraid to take on fate
and stare it in the eye.
You are invulnerable!
Your pulse will last forever.
Surging through your waters,
to the echo of your heartbeat.

Paul Kelly

Seed Time

Sowing the seeds of peace
now and forever after.
Whose image do we bear?
Who is our earthly master?

Do we sow in fear, in hatred,
in dissension with our neighbour?
Reaping a bitter harvest
despite our well-meant labour?
Do we sow in condescension,
in social, national pride?
Then wonder why our harvest
in wormy rot has died?

Do we sow the seeds of peace
in our own thoughts first of all;
then the crops we reap each day
though weak perhaps and small –
sowed in turn, will gender
the mightiest harvest ever;
feeding the nation's hunger
as we work the fields together.
As we work with love and laughter,
reaping the crops of peace
now and forever after.

Diana S Morcom

War Or Roses

Lancaster of York which house will reign?
The Plantagenets seek the throne for gain
While emblems of white fly amid blazons of red
Adorned by our rose, soars the standard ahead.

Shall the flags hang low for the valiant loss?
Another victory marked by a wooden cross
Or will banners strewn with shield and plume
Rise high to the pride of our rose in bloom?

Alas! Warwick's envious eyes behold
The crown with pearls and sceptre gold
But Kingmaker's triumph can never steal
The riches that our rose cannot conceal.

Its kingdom made by a mightier hand
Than sword of state or royal command
It captures the warmth of nature's sweet grace
Our rose seeks the purest of gold to embrace.

So many petals, so red and so white
Lie broken and torn in the arrow's cruel flight
As the gift of each passing clouds bequest
Falls to our rose, our regal crest.

John Carter

Choices

Looking back along my life I see a highway
Only measured by the age I am today
With voices calling out from every byway
Do they lead me or do I really know my way?
Different pathways, many choices and selection,
Who's to say what makes me choose which path to take
In the mirror you don't always see reflection
Just the glare of your omission or mistake.

Regrets and ruefulness are not of this equation
My chosen path I travel come what may,
I pursue it to its natural conclusion
I may even lose direction on the way
Wisdom tints my life in manageable doses
Confidence is loaned, don't take it to extreme
Decisions made and rightly one supposes
Mistakes are never easy to redeem.

Life, work and leisure, people and occasions
Bring joy and sadness, enjoyment and regret
My life a train and these are all the stations
Some stops not worth recalling so forget.
These days when I look back along that highway
The only thing I'll hear is my own voice
And it shouldn't come as much of a surprise to hear it whisper
Keep going on this road, it's been your choice.

M Catherine Huggett

Old Man At The Pier

He was stood there in dated attire
Gazing across the old bay
Living each ancient day
Crooked stature and lost desire

Back bent feather ruffled coat shaken to reveal a huddled mind
His frail grip on the rail, ancient clawed hand brown but for wrinkles within
So much has changed he said through his white grin
This was our town you know she's gone now and memories are kind

I stared through salt air mist blurring his reflection
The pier's extended he said, a hundred or more feet
A little appendage of life to make it complete
He's patiently lingering for some chance of connection

He thanked me for being awakened
Trapped in the moment he dare not leave
I walk away as I watch him grieve
Didn't turn back lest I be mistaken.

John Foster

Nightingale

My fragile
Body
Racked
With pain,
Another night that
I couldn't sleep
Again.
Lonely,
As all around
Others slumbered.
Then I heard
A sound;
The sweetest
Birdsong
Loud and clear,
Reminded me,
Father,
That You
Are always near.

In the darkness
He sang for me,
My body weak,
My spirit free.
As the dawn
Slowly came,
So did sleep –
And I praised
Your Name.

Geri Laker

A tiny drop of water can make you stop and think
That such a simple entity can provide such words as drink
I'm grateful for this simple thing that makes us all alive
Without it in this perilous world I doubt we would survive
I admire the garden in the morning sun
And the springtime rain that follows short after
Once again the water nourishes life relieves it and sustains it
A tiny drop can make a limp, lifeless flower bloom once again
A tiny drop can make it stand proud, tall and strong
A tiny drop can quench the thirst of the smallest child
The smallest cup can clean away a scuff or graze
The smallest cup can cool and refresh your pets
The smallest cup can make fun in the heat
The simplest thing that we take for granted is our life
The simplest thing gives us energy and fun
The simplest thing that refreshes and cools
Every night before I sleep I give thanks for this water
And the world that it keeps I hope it will never ever run out
And the cruellest word appears such as drought
I dance in the garden under the hose in the sweet summer heat
Rejoicing in the cooling spray of water
Thinking once again how glad I am that we have it
And how much better I feel now I'm cool
For the simplest thing I'm grateful and cool.

Barbara Scott

The Brooch

When I was ill with cancer,
Receiving cursed, cold chemotherapy,
My John gave me a beautiful
Vintage brooch for Valentine's day.
The art deco diamante sparkling
Heart-shaped brooch has a looped hoop
Of thirteen faux pearls
Graduating in size beginning
In the middle of the heart.
On the back of the brooch,
Which is silver, Marvella,
The designer's name, is stamped.
At the time John called me
Baldilocks, as I had no hair.
I wore the brooch on a black turban,
Almost part of the Bloomsbury set.
Sixteen months later, I am well.
My hair has cute chemo curls,
I am content and strong.
John and I are happily married.
The brooch is a symbol of
Enduring love and hope.
I treasure its warm joy.

Mary May Robertson

Take Time

Walk slow like the tortoise,
And tall like the giraffe,
Along the lanes of life,
Do not forget to laugh,
Take in all that natural beauty,
Gently stroll along,
Observing trees and flowers,
While birds sing their song,
There is more to life than rushing,
Here, there and everywhere,
Have a look in the mirror,
You will also find beauty there.
You are God's special creation
He made you quite unique,
Trust in Him and in those who love you,
You will find all the riches from above,
For the greatest gift in all the world,
Is the gift of unconditional love.

Terry Gilvin

Daily Reflections

Fate

A coincidence, a chance appearance
As I walked to the gate
At that split second, not a moment
Would I hesitate . . .

My clothes I'd changed, my hair I'd tied
Sunglasses I'd misplaced
My door I opened, sunshine blinded
The eyes which met my face

The door could have been opened
Twenty seconds in advance
And then I would never have created quite a chance
So a coincidence as he appeared, as I walked to the gate
Meant my life had turned a corner, thanks to fate.

Emma Hawkesford

God's Little Acre

I love
the unkempt beauty
of this quiet corner -
God's Little Acre -
especially spring harvest-time
when crocuses, wind-blown
this way and that
mingle their mauves and white
amidst the uneven grass
with scattered clumps
of fragrant primroses.
The 'little, humble celandine'
holds its own, too,
it's velvet yellow outshining
windswept daffodils.
Here squirrels play.
To watch their flight
from branch to branch
chasing each other
through the tangled mass
of overhanging foliage
is to glimpse
playfulness
at the heart of all things,
to perceive joy
in the carefree abundance
of creation.

Rosemary Wells

Untitled

The human foot –
a miracle
We are crude in
our creations
Save our actions with
each other
We are capable of great
beauty in
our dealings with
each other –
a kind, timely word
the building of love
faithfulness
Yes here we excel
and with ourselves
us alone
When we cover
deserts and mountain ranges
in our greatness and
purity of thought
our great strides, our
bravery, our vision
the gods of wood and
stone are ashamed
when with a correct spirit
we stride to change or
build or fly.

Paul Barron

Faith Changes Everything

Faith changes everything
Light *'embraces'* - a smile is born
Faith changes everything
A soul is stirred, no more forlorn

A light so welcoming
And its touch so warm
Faith gives birth to joy in you
Your spirit dances - is set free
'A happy tear is shed in thankful prayer'

Faith changes everything
Shadows lift, colour floods in
Faith changes everything
Days are clearer, nights more calm

Faith eyes fixed on God above
Trusting eyes *bathed in peace*
Lost in praise and wonder
Of His majesty and grace
Knowing that His way will always be the best

Faith laughs in the face of night
Amid evil and haunting doubt
What a power surrounding -
Within and without!

Faith - *'A ship to sail upon'*
Guiding safely in to shore
Faith - a strong foundation
Changing lives for evermore

Isabel Taylor

Let Your Mercy Shine

Dear Lord I'm frequently unkind
Help me humility to find
In others goodness help me see
And let Your mercy shine on me

In thoughtless haste, just passing by
Help me to recognise a cry
Of pain of sadness to be free
And let Your mercy shine on me

In talk of someone else's sin
Do I too joyfully in
Help me of malice to be free
And let Your mercy shine on me

You've given me hearing, sight and voice
So many blessings I rejoice
To use them wisely is my plea
So let Your mercy shine on me.

Enid Gill

Knowing You

An aspect of creation I have come to know
As I look to the heavens and see the rainbow
I am grateful for being a friend whom I'm yet to know
Looking down to the ground
Feeling the heat under my feet
I realise this friendship is incomplete

You constantly give
I constantly take
A balance is needed to avoid heartaches
With an open hand you satisfy all desires
I look at my life - it's all pleasures

You never burden with your commands
So I need to readjust my stance
From creation until now you have always provided
So my friend I'll take the time
To learn about you
To have a future
With friendship in view

Angela Nevo Hopkins

Fun!

20th February

Life's too short to sit in the corner,
Not saying anything.
Instead, get up, grab the microphone,
And sing, sing, sing!

If everyone is dancing,
Don't look and say, 'No chance!'
Instead, get on the dance floor,
And dance, dance, dance!

Let your arms wave above,
Let your bum wiggle.
Let yourself just lose control,
And giggle, giggle, giggle!

And when you get tired of doing those things,
And you need to rest for a while,
Do something that isn't tiring,
Smile, smile, smile!

Mary-Clare Newsham (12)

Dawn Chorus

Fingers of light
Stealthy and silent
Streak darkened sky,
While mortals still sleep.

Raising his baton
The heavenly conductor
Signals the soloist:
The concert begins.

Notes sweet and clear
From the throat of the blackbird,
Lead feathered choristers
In paeans of praise

Melodic perfection,
In perfect harmony,
Reaching crescendo:
Dies slowly away.

Invisible hands
Peel back curtains of darkness,
Nature exults
At another new day.

And only man, slumbering,
Fails to applaud.

Jeanne Selley

There Is Life After A Car Crash

She nearly died
But she survived
Many of her bones were broken
But not her spirit
She was in hospital for months
But she did come home
She goes out in a wheelchair
But she is not bedridden
She has little memory of the past
But then the past cannot hurt her
She has her nasty moods
But she doesn't mean them
Her old friends have forgotten her
But that is their loss
She cannot go to work
But we have the pleasure of her company
She has many scars
But we can help them heal
She often flounders
We can be there to pick up
She cannot cope with pressure
We can iron out life's stresses for her
We now judge shops by their wheelchair access
But we can all still shop
She has a totally different life
But she does have a life
We have a totally different life
But together with our daughter we do have a life
Life is very precious and we can all learn
To adapt our lives to fit our circumstances.

Cherry Somers-Dowell

My Motto

Always live each day as if it were your last
Don't worry about the future, reflect on the past.
Reliving the joy and the fun shared with friends
Following life's path wherever it bends.

For the less able, give them some of your time
Brighten their life with a funny little rhyme.
Go to the shops, or help with a difficult task
Offer your help, because they will not ask.

Put a smile on your face as you walk into town
Don't let the wind or rain get you down.
The rain is necessary for our beautiful land
Feel sorry for the people who live on desert sand.

Most of all, share laughter and love
And thank God for the sun up above.
Use your talents to make the most of your life
Sharing and caring will overcome strife.

Lynne Walden

Sleepless Night

In the night
> . . . darkness seems darker
> . . . time never-ending
> . . . problems loom larger
> . . . pain more intense

But
> . . . find God in the darkness
> . . . His presence is constant
> . . . use time for reflection
> . . . your soul to renew

So
> . . . transform this frustration
> . . . when sleep flees unbidden
> . . . relax in the knowledge
> . . . He still cares for you

Then
> . . . gently but firmly
> . . . re-focus your vision
> . . . let peace flood your being
> . . . you'll sleep like a child.

Mary A Garrick

Untitled

How like the swan
Looking on
Into a material world
Whilst in habitat
Their world
Our world
A reflection of the other
How different
Stark in places
Yet blending in
Among historical buildings
Who allowed their presence
Undisturbed or perturbed
By us
On the other side
Of reality.

Deborah Hall

Neighbours

I planned to buy a country home
When I was old and grey.
I knew I would be all alone,
But I'd enjoy each day.

Yet no one knows what lies ahead
My schemes all went astray.
Now I am in an 'old folks' flat,
And this is where I'll stay.

No need to say that I'm content,
You'll hear that in my voice.
It's such a caring atmosphere
I'm happy with my choice.

The folk around me are not rich,
But we have wealth untold.
For helping hands and kindly deeds
Are worth far more than gold.

I have good friends about me
For a chat or cup of tea.
We sometimes go on theatre trips
Or a day out by the sea.

We walk up to the local shop
Or catch the bus to town.
There's always someone near at hand
If ever I feel down.

I may not have a roof of thatch
Or roses round my door,
But I have friends on every side,
And who could ask for more?

Katie Simpson

Make Up

I see me in a mirror
A face I've seen before
But now it's full of confidence
As life opens another door.
So many paths to Heaven
Though some are full of pain
But every tear that's shed this way
Brings strength and hope again.
So as we journey onward,
Upward we must go
And remember every wrinkle
Experience
The looking glass shows!

Lyn Sandford

Peace

A cloudless sky with pallid moonlight filled
And stars that seem to be by winter chilled;
Fields and hedgerows gleam with sparkling frost
A time when cares of day might well be lost.

Sounds of night, nocturnal hunters prowl
Barking fox, the distant screech of owl,
No wind to stir the ghostly barren trees
Let this stillness set the troubled mind at ease.

For if by turbulent thoughts you are oppressed,
Then strive this way to calm the troubled breast;
Quietly commune with nature undemanding,
You may find God's peace, beyond all understanding.

Norrie Ferguson

Come Let Us Walk In Spring's Path

Spring . . .
The annual resurgence of life
A tide which cannot be stopped
Snowdrops nudging through the snow
Daisies smiling on the frosted lawn
Come wind or sleet spring dances on
Undaunted in the face of every foe

Spring seems so fragile, so demure
Heavenly scented, so unsure
Pastel pinks, translucent blues
Interspersed with yellow hues
Delicate spring tiptoes her way
Leaving footprints that are here to stay

Spring has come! Winter must flee
To the dark recesses of a dying year
Life now pulsates; the voice of nature awakens
Bird songs and buzzings of insect musicians
Singing one song
Heralding victory over what's gone!

Olympia Barczynska

Trust

I had a problem and I came to you.
I wanted advice only a father could give.
You loaned me your precious car.
Your arm around my shoulder.
You are my inspiration to live.
I feel secure when I am with you.
You never betray a confidence.
You listen and store in your brain,
A wealth of common sense.
You say I can count on you whatever time of day.
Dad! For what you have done for me,
Believe these words, I will repay.

Patricia Ainscough

God's World

God gave us the flowers that bloom in the spring,
And the tiny birds that whistle and sing,
He gave us the sunshine, a rainbow and showers,
A wonderful world, made by God's mighty power.

He gave us the mountains, the rivers and streams,
And woodlands and valleys that look so serene,
He gave man the knowledge, to write music and hymns,
So when we all gather, can sing praises to Him.

He gave us the seas and a moon that shines light,
That shows us the way, when we walk out at night,
He gave us each other to love and to cherish,
Gave us His promise, that none will e'er perish.

A world that is bounteous, enough for us all,
Is being spoiled by man, whose greed ruins all,
A world full of beauty, so wondrous and bright,
Is slowly becoming a world full of plight.

This beautiful world which God gave to us,
Needs care and attention, not abuse and distrust,
So just make the time to sit and reflect,
Each thing God created that turned out perfect.

Jean Bruton

Heralds

Snowdrops, loveliest of flowers,
Brightening winter's darkest hours.
Carpets of green and white
Spreading pleasure, sheer delight.
Undeterred by stormy weather,
Brave battalions band together,
Resist attempts to mow them down,
Steadfastly stand their ground.
Delicate, yet so strong,
Nodding heads ring out spring's song.

Sue Cann

Faith In Prayer

When Heaven ignores your prayer
and teardrops fill your eyes
worry clouds gather swiftly
then a cloudburst fills the skies.

Let God guide you onward
in your time of need
use your faith in prayer
and the Lord will take the lead.

The dawn may bring answers
to problems of your day
the world will appear brighter
when the sun has shone its ray.

Alex Branthwaite

A Prayer For Lent And Springtime

(With a response)

Lord of green and growing spring –
    Whose gentle power
Waylays us in an unexpected flower –
    Today we bring
Garlands of mingled hope and fear;
    But You are here,
Though fears prevail and hopes are few:
    God of springtime, make us new.

Christ of sad and solemn Lent,
    We watch You go
Towards a cruel trial whose end we know;
    And so present
New wreaths of joy to crown Your pain:
    For You will reign.
Such is our faith – so strangely true:
    God of springtime, make us new.

Almighty Victor, Easter King –
    Who played and won,
And proved that love sustains the stars and sun –
    We dare to bring
Our fragile lives for grace to fill
    With glad goodwill;
And speak, in simplest love, with You.
    God of springtime, make us new.

John Coutts

Around Me

After the rain comes the drought.
Caught up in and captured, this comfort I can't live without.
And the warmth which envelopes my soul,
Which soothes my whole being, reminds me creation is whole.
Inside the wind is the breeze,
It flies all around me and takes my concerns far away.
Then I'm down on the ground on my knees,
Giving thanks for just living, for being a part of this day.
Because regardless of how my mind feels,
And though my life is the chaos of overgrown, under-walked grass,
Slowly, my aura heals,
As I grasp that creation does nothing but live just to laugh.

Thomas Bissell

Seen From A Conservatory Window

As I sit on my window seat,
I look down the garden and I see
The purple bush of lavateria sweet,
Nearby yellow sunflowers waving merrily.

My eyes then turn to hebe sweet
The pink of small geraniums close by
And then I see a hydrangea great
All this beauty is pleasing to the eye.

But I majored on pots this year,
The scent of begonias fills the air,
With busy lizzies then petunias appear:
And all this beauty needs special care.

Our God is the Creator, we give Him praise
Each flower so bright owes existence to Him.
I wonder at Him and all His ways
His power is limitless - all glory to Him.

M G Worth

God's Morning

Lord I rise and greet the morning,
Then I fall upon my knees
In thankfulness that You are there
To answer all my needs,
Lead me through the day before me
Take my hand and be my guide
I can never fail or stumble
When You're walking at my side

Teach me all Your ways of goodness
Show me how to live for You
Then sweet thoughts of You will colour
Everything I say or do
Then when night again encroaches
And I lay me down to rest
I shall have no fear of darkness
When with Your love I am ever blest.

Then I'll rise again tomorrow
Strong in faith to face the day
Knowing that my pain and sorrow
By Your grace will fade away
So on every bright new morning
I'll awake to worship You
Safe within Your loving kindness
I will be forever true.

Barbara Scriven

Responding To Love

I shall say about the one I love, tho with great difficulty.
I shall say it with deep reverence because He loves the likes of me.
He is the smile that often plays around a mouth once upside down.
He is the twinkle in the hazel eyes that used to wear a frown.
He is the melody that cannot cease, it pours from deep within.
He is the butterflies I often feel because He has freed me from my sin.
He is the tapping of the dancing feet, He is the giggle behind the hand.
He is my laughter and my happiness, He is the One who understands.
He knows I've been so lonely, also knew I had no love.
He came because Love is His name, Love came from high above.
He is Love and therefore pure so to dust He could not go.
The light of love shines ever on so that the likes of me could know.
Could know where there is no loneliness when you said you need His love.
In a second away the emptiness as He shines down from above.
Love placed a vessel in my hand 'tis a cup full to overflowing.
Love leads me gently by the hand and describes where we are going.
He is leading me to Heaven where no tears are never known.
He tells me it is paradise where hatred is not shown.
He says there shall be dangers as He leads me to His home.
But tho I meet with enemies I shall not be alone.
So onwards, on to paradise with the One who has my heart.
This is He, He is my beloved who from me will never part.
'Tis truly a wonderful journey with still quite a way to go.
Life's encyclopaedia is set before me for there is much to know and show.

O Lord O' mine . . .

Rosie Hues

Happiness

Happiness is a frail and tender thing,
A gentle whisper on the still, soft air;
Too fragile for the grasp of eager hands,
Too slender for the heavy cloak of care.

Doubt casts his shadow and the thunderclouds
Obscure from view the glory of the sun.
Forgotten are the promises once made,
And all the webs of hope and faith once spun.

Like quicksilver it's there and then is gone,
So rare to find, so swift to pass away,
Leaving behind a harder, colder world,
Enveloped in a shroud of misty grey.

This precious thread has strength unseen, untried -
Awhile the winds of patience softly blow
To cast away the storm clouds from the sky -
And happiness will braver, stronger grow.

Caroline Byron-Johnson

Faith, Hope And Charity

8th March

Faith, hope and charity,
Three words we should embrace
But sometimes they get lost,
Gone, without a trace

Faith, hope and charity,
Inspirational expressions,
Hold them in our hearts,
To eliminate depressions

Faith, hope and charity,
A trio of fine words,
Old fashioned values some may say,
But words that should be heard

Faith, hope and charity,
Meaningful and deep,
Retain these values in our hearts,
When awake and whilst asleep

Faith, hope and charity,
Sometimes these words lie dormant,
If we believe in them
We all will have less torment

That's why I still have faith,
There's still hope left in me
To show the kindness in my heart
Will mean there's charity.

Diane Crouch

Beautiful Child

Born out of circumstance
Long time ago.
Beautiful child
As mothers well know.

You grew up
With a struggle.
We fought and we cried,
All that behind us,
I'm glad we survived.

As time goes by
You too will know
The pains I once suffered
Long time ago.

Be happy my child
Wherever you go.
I'm just your mother
From long time ago.

Susan Draper

Follow That Path

Sometimes we need to be reminded of the path that we chose
And when we are led astray then we forget that road
But a little help and a guiding hand will see us through
It will put us back on the path that we chose to do
We need to have faith and hope in the good Lord above
Because He will show us the way and send us His love
We need to have trust that God's way is so right
Without these things the path is out of our sight
So trust in God for He will send us all of His love
He will not falter but will send it from high above
The path you chose will soon appear in your sight
And then you will know that God does get it right
He never makes a mistake He knows just what to do
So believe in Him and you will also know it too.

Margaret Ward

Lord Help The Grieving

O Lord grant me peace of heart in all things this day.
As troubled waters rise above me, please show me the way.
Let not my soul be cast down but see all things through Your eyes
For You alone are the supreme God only wise.
I love You Lord for You are my maker although the storms still come
For who else but through You do streams of living water run?
Forgive me Lord for the doubts that arise,
For I know that they are nought but lies.
When help would seem so far away
I feel at a loss, then comes another day.
As the sunshine comes to dry away my tears
And Your Spirit ever near to take away my fears.
But my heart still aches as I hear loved ones weep,
For they are still going through waters deep.
Please comfort them o God I pray.
Put Your loving arms around them this day.
Let them forever feel Your presence near
And dear Lord please take away their inmost fear.

Anna Powell

Stepping About

By stepping in and stepping out
I'm finding what it's all about

Each time I'm born again
I learn the lesson between joy and pain

Stepping in and stepping out
Is finding out what it's about

Stuart Waldron

Nature's Lesson

Whenever I feel lonely, whenever I feel sad,
I look at nature's beauty, it always makes me glad,
It matters not the season or what the time of day,
Mother Nature in her bounty has only this to say,
'Child, cast off your lonely gloom and end all bitter strife,
Wonders great and wonders small make up the joy of life,
Rugged mountains tall and grim, the daisies at your feet,
All between, my gift to you whilst day and night still meet,
Look and listen with your heart and let your spirit soar,
Life's delight I freely give, yet you can have still more,
Smile again at all who pass, let your 'hello' be bright,
You will find your spirit lift and life is full of light.'

M G Smith

Happy As A Sand Boy

Looking out on a Sri Lankan dawn
From my comfortable existence and over the lawns
The sand boys dredge up sand and dreams
From the Mahaweli riverbed where life it seems
Has stood still for centuries or more
This simple existence from the river floor
Through happy eyes they toil all day
In mist and heat for a pittance of pay
Yet we have a lot to learn
From these eyes that do not burn
With envy, greed or wistful longing
Their inner peace and sense of belonging
Is a lesson to all bent solely on material gain
These happy boys steeped in Buddha's flame
The teaching of a lifetime's joy
Has made them happy as sand boys.

Peter Ellis

Thoughts

With some good thoughts I start the day
But then with time my thoughts do stray
Sometimes they are good and
Sometimes they are bad
And some I wish I never had
I plan to do some good for others
But then again I never bother
If one could change their way of life
If one could change this sad world's strife
The wars that never seem to end
The will of nations that never bend
They fight and kill without a thought
And then forget the pain they wrought
The desolation at their hand
The cruelty of man to man
But what can one lone person do
To change the way this world grew
A lone voice in the wilderness
Would not be heard among this mess
So now I leave the way to God
The path in life that must be trod
For Him there is a reason why
For Him is not to do or die
I ask Him to guide me on my way
And help me live from day to day
Most days I know I fail the test
But then God knows I do my best
If I never hurt by rule or might
Another person's human right
If I never take someone's good name
Or make someone in life ashamed

But maybe by a gift from God
Can help another's life road trod
And give to someone else the bliss
Of a little joy and happiness.

Eithne McCrossan

Untitled

Our hearts are special places
where memories are kept
to somehow bring us comfort
when all our tears are wept

They're full of special moments
of times we've laughed and cried
and simply thinking of them
brings loved ones to our side

And though those loved ones may have passed
their memory never parts
and we can see them any time we want
by looking in our hearts.

Sian Lewis-Yardley

At World's End

A home there . . .
Trumpet vines before the original
Front door of French, now red latex behind
Two gigantic slabs of stone. Think of hoisting
Such slabs, the effort of maintenance, that
Farmhouse so ramshackle the walls had
Growing pains.

Now there is such stillness, ageless
In the leaving, the departure of children,
Such a resonant hush that any creak
Signifies love still.

But was it expected, the breakage, the sweet
Flotsam of blossoms? I wake from dreams

Carrying all this inside, like those dolls
Within dolls, the replicated kernel, a walnut
Adinfin . . .
Such, the chambers of our hearts . . .

So the home at World's End is world's
Beginning once more. Again we are there,
Full of knowledge that these rooms, these
Beings made us, hands clasped as an arch

Amen shaped.

Stephen Mead

Beryl's Prayer

Lord You know the feelings of our inmost hearts,
The good things and the bad,
You know when we are happy, and also when we're sad.
We bring to You our burdens, with You alone we share,
We know that You will listen and answer every prayer.
As we tread this path called life along the rugged way,
We know that You are with us to help us day by day.

B Norris

A Sea Of Blue

Blue as far as the eye can see
Beautiful irises dressed to impress
Tall and straight, bold and blue
Swaying in the morning breeze

What beauty we find in a flower
Delicate and fresh as the morning dew
Striking colours with that hint of yellow
How beautiful this flower in spring

A wonderful greeting each morning we see
Its brightness delicate as a butterfly
Touch a petal very softly
It has a feel of silk

The iris.

Carole A Cleverdon

Friends

Thank You Lord for faithful friends,
More precious than purest gold.
Their comforting and steadfast love
Beyond costliest treasures sold.

In troubled times they hold us fast,
Uplift us with their care,
Their thoughtfulness protects us
And heals us with their prayer.

In good times too we need them,
To share our joy and cheer,
For peace of mind and a cheerful heart
And friendship always near.

So praise the Lord and give thanks
For dear friends that we love,
Constant and true despite all our faults,
They are a blessing from above.

Joan Gorton

Son Bathing

Basking in Your warmth
I rest in Your presence
Soaking up rays of joy and peace

The sea that laps gently
An ocean of love
Washing over my soul

My spirit soars to Your Heaven
You are beautiful

Lightning is a taste of Your strength
Thunder just a whisper

Gentle as a butterfly
You draw close

For You made me
And You know me.

Ruth M Ellett

Lost Eden?

Trees rousing from their winter sleep
Stretching forth shoots and leaves,
Brown turns to green, the eyes' delight,
Crystal air breathes new life.

Streams from their icy prison freed
Like children, rush to play
And bubble, blabbering over stones
And threading down ravines.

Birds find their voices, dawn awakes
By choral charm enhanced,
The little, busy, fluttering days
Spent building nests and bowers.

Snowdrops emerge in modest white,
Pendant heads shyly swing,
Followed by sunny celandines,
Violets cushioned in green.

Bold daffodils push up their heads,
Skirts ruffling in the breeze;
Down in the moss, primroses lie,
Pale echoes of the sun.

Over the world, troubles extend,
Conflicts, injustice, pain;
Man's will, not God's, seems to prevail,
Children again betrayed.

But beauty in an English spring
Tells us His love still holds
And this rich garden shows us yet
How Eden might have been.

Joy Jenkins

Today As Always

(For Mam, Brenda Margaret Frowen)

Yesterday we held your hand
Today as always you hold our hearts
Yesterday our tears fell like rain
Today you wiped them all away
Yesterday we talked
Today you still listen
Yesterday we spoke your name in sadness
Today we smiled as we talked of you
Yesterday you embraced us
Today we still feel the warmth
Yesterday we thought you'd be with us forever
Today we heard you whisper you always will be

Jan Maissen

Spring

It is the first day of spring,
Such a wonderful thing,
A time for all things new to be born,
A time for the thoughts of bitterness, from winter, to be torn.

Newborn spring lambs leaping peacefully through the tall blades of grass,
Fluffy, white and innocent, a picture which throughout spring will last,
Chasing the first few butterflies, while they flutter through the air,
Spreading their pure beauty everywhere.

Fluffy spring chicks hatch from their eggs,
Jumping playfully on their tiny little legs,
Golden-yellow like the sun,
Sweetly chirping telling of the love for their mum.

Little buds popping from the trees,
Soon to flourish into fruit, flowers and leaves,
Beautiful buds blooming from the bulbs,
Getting ready for the summer when the flowers will brighten every field, forest,
wood and wold.

It is the first day of spring,
Such a wonderful thing,
A time for all things new to be born,
A time for the thoughts of bitterness, from winter, to be torn.

Kate Shaw (15)

Gleam Of Dawn

A period of time during the hour
And signs of growth appear to flower
Coloured sky as morning breaks
Reflects brightness across the lakes

The sharpness of the sky above
There to enjoy and to love
A time to be out with the morning dew
And a graceful breeze as it gently blew

Finding a track along the route
There to satisfy and suit
Guided by the signs of light
Given to follow after dark night

Appearance of life within the trees
As birds sing their chorus in the breeze
Reminding me of a book I read
And put my trust for One to lead

A path to follow through the morn
'Like the first gleam of dawn'
Becoming brighter through the day
And progress found with no delay.

James Stephen Thompson

Lovers In The Bulbs

In the sparkling spring,
    bulbs awaken in the breeze:
Purple, pink and white hyacinths,
    cylinders of little blooms;
White and yellow daffodils,
    stars around yellow and orange horns;
Tiny purple grape hyacinths,
    clusters of hanging beads;
White Easter lilies,
    now wilting in new life;
Fetal tulips still folded,
    ready to burst in unfolding splendour –
All bedded on spiky green leaves
    full of energy
guided by the sun.

On the ground of this Faerie Forest,
    moist and rich,
    hidden and shaded,
    from the Daystar
was asleep a fairy couple,
    embracing, entangled under a leaf.
Long after the Dawn
    when Faerie plays,
Long before the Dusk
    when Faerie awakens,
The lovers dream as one
    in their own world of mystery.

John A Mills

New Spring Day

Spring is wakening this old world again
with violets and primroses down the lane
Mrs Robin has prepared her small nest
and Mrs Wren where only she knows best
Mrs Swallow has shaped her mud nest as well
but where Mrs Skylark nests . . . I won't tell . . .
As the cuckoo calls and tiny lambs play
it's great to be alive this new spring day.

Valerie Ovais

God's Love

God's love is welcoming
God's love is everlasting
God's love is eternal
God's love is pure
God's love is filled with joy
God's love is the same yesterday,
Today and forever
God's love is more precious
Than rubies or diamonds
God's love is unconditional
God's love is hopeful
God's love is uplifting
God's love is higher than the heavens
God's love is long suffering
God's love bears all
God's love is merciful
God's love is forgiving
God's love is complete
God's love is perfect

Berenice Healy

The Good Friday Tree

What does Good Friday mean to me?
Such an ugly cross from a beautiful tree:
Its branches chopped, its beauty gone,
so that they could murder God's only Son.

That tree like Jesus grew from a seed,
to kill them both there was no need:
Such a dreadful shame, such a tragedy,
they both were stripped of their dignity.

I'm sure that tree cried on that day,
as it cradled Him close while His life slipped away:
But now in Heaven it grows anew,
with branches that reach out to me and you.

It seems to be calling 'Reach out and see,
the meaning of life grows strong like a tree':
When you think you are falling and need some support,
hang on to its branches and make a new start.

On the third day Jesus rose from the grave
to return to His Father in Heaven:
His work was complete He had given His all,
His life that our sins be forgiven.

Don't let your Saviour have died in vain,
mortally wounded and racked with pain:
Offer Him your love and repentance too,
and one day in Heaven you'll grow anew.

Brenda Nash

Easter Song

Clouds - heavy, swirling, grey, black.
Hills - craggily etched against the sky,
    white streaks, snow.
There is no joy in the sky;
    no laughter from the sun.
Foreboding, stillness, anticipation . . .

Why, Lord? Why?
Why do You love me so much?
What have I done to deserve such favour?

There You are, on the cross,
    outstretched for me,
        crying, calling, bleeding, dying.
Gasping in agony,
    pouring out blood.
Still, so still, utter stillness.

The storm breaks,
    thunder, lightning,
        dark, dark, dark.
Slowly, slowly, inch by inch,
    light pierces the dark
spreads across the sky,
    eclipses the dark
        into a panoply of colour . . .
Light, life, mystery, *resurrection.*

Jesus lives,
He is my Lord and Saviour,
Risen Christ,
    My life, my hope, my song.

Pamela Murray

Life

Buds tightly closed;
hermetically sealed
against anything that might destroy.
Until, against all odds,
the most delicate of flowers appears
petals opening to the life-giving warmth of the sun.

Egg shells, strong as iron;
armour plated
against anything that might devour.
Until, against all odds,
the gaping beak breaks through,
gasping for life-giving air.

Tomb, stone cold;
sealed tight
against anyone that might plunder.
Until, against all odds,
bursting through death itself
the life-giver lives again.

Ruth Walker

Easter Joy

Jesus is risen!
The tomb is now bare;
They look - and they see -
He is not there!
For He walks in the garden
Of beauty and peace;
Free from all suffering,
Anguish and grief.

He walks in the sunshine;
But some will not know,
Yet we - we are happy -
Our hearts are aglow.
For we know the story
We who believe,
And can bask in the glory,
That He is alive.

Alive like each new birth,
That comes into being -
The calf and the cattle
That each day we are seeing.
Each stunning tulip
So fresh when in bloom,
Rises in abundance -
Like Christ from the tomb;
To beautify for all,
Who tread upon this Earth,
Like a flicker of sun
On a stallion's girth.

Wendy Watkin

To Witness The Sky

A wave of happiness rushes through your veins,
From your toes to your finger tips,
A blur of happy haze,
A smile smoothes over your cherry-red lips,
Like a cool watermelon, minus the pips.

For today you looked up and witnessed the sky,
From your window you stared out and left the inside behind,
No need to shiver, nor let out a sigh,
The sun shone down and lit up your life,
Leaving you glowing, fresh and revived.

Katie Cheetham

Life's Reserve

Attain for me, all life's reserve,
Convey to be,
In all, I conserve,
Keep me from harm,
In this life, that I live,
Give me Your strength, Lord,
In the power of, forgive,
Just for today,
Have a place, on its time,
To honour, convey and bestow,
Give me Your wisdom,
To see all that's due,
Remind me, oh Lord,
That our thoughts are with You,
Those deals with another,
Be they sister or brother,
May each have a role,
To their part,
Of render, all stories,
That add up to might,
The concerns for us, hurries,
Can so come, in night,
But tender our thoughts Lord,
Be their keeping, with You,
Forsaking all others,
What we say, be of true.

Hugh Campbell

Words Of Faith And Hope

God give me a heart
That's kind and true,
Give me faith to walk with You,
Give me courage to see things through,
Hope and strength from You to pursue.
Whatever path my feet may tread
May You be always at my head.
When troubles knock at my door
You may open it and love outpour.
When I am weak, You are strong
That Your love for us all
Lasts our whole life long.
You are there for our every need
So raise your eyes to the skies
God will hear your prayer
And listen, take heed,
Comfort you in times of need
Have faith, believe all will be well,
God is there, time will tell.

I G Corbett

Let Go Of The Past

Do past memories ever trouble, or perhaps even haunt you?
Without a doubt, at unexpected moments, they very often do!
Simply because we're meant to learn,
Many lessons from all of this –
To enable us to live a life Blessed with Heavenly Bliss.
Though we may never understand
The sacrifices we're asked to make –
Take it for Granted, and just Believe,
You're doing them for our dear Lord's Sake.

M Ross

Paths Of Life

To a new friend
Thank you for accepting
Helping hands.
For it makes my life worthwhile
To be useful!
The kitchen is so friendly
It has such a homely feel
When we come in muddy and tired
From gardening
To steaming pots of tea
And ploughman's lunch
Spread on the kitchen table
With Irish setters at our feet!
Perhaps things happen for a reason
And people's paths are meant to cross . . .
Funny thing these paths
Some folk are just so nice
You feel you've known them
All your life!

E Osmond

What Is Life For?

'What is life for?' I ask myself time and time again.
For two people it's never the same.
The only thing in common is that we're all born to die,
it's that bit in the middle that concerns you and I.

Life is a lottery - you win or you lose,
You're one of life's haves or have nots, it's not yours to choose.
The haves go from strength to strength, nothing stops them
Whilst the have nots are hit back time and time again.

'What is life for?' I ask myself a lot.
Can the haves do something for the have nots?
Many have tried, sometimes in vain,
but at least they have tried to ease the pain.
Others look on and spare not a thought
for the poor and suffering and care not a jot.

On our rebirth will the lottery change
and the haves become have nots through lessons gained?
Maybe they will, only time will reveal
but the mystery of life depends on the spin of the wheel.

Anne Jenkins

Memories

There are certain times throughout the year
Our thoughts turn to loved ones no longer here
It's sometimes hard to keep the tears at bay
On what would have been their special day
From the sadness of death we still feel the pain
When loved ones die our lives are never the same
Their separation leaves such a big hole
Grief overwhelms us tearing at our soul
We often dwell on words left unsaid
It's better to focus on the good times instead
Memories sustain us when we're feeling sad
Remembering the love and special times we've had
Love doesn't end when our loved ones depart
We carry that love with us etched in our heart
Love helps us to cope when our grief's hard to bear
When we're weighed down by sorrow and despair
The love shared together still lives on through you
Hold onto that love to carry you through
The sad and the low times, the grief and the tears
All brought to the surface at special times of the year
It's because of their love it's so hard when we part
So cherish your memories, holding them close to your heart.

Karen Wilson

Daily Reflections

Almost There

You're almost there,
It's almost done,
The battle fought,
The dreams soon won.

You're almost through
The work and pain.
The sun will shine
Above the rain.

You're almost past
The worry and fear.
True happiness
Is drawing near.

You're almost done,
So one more prayer.
Just one deep breath.
You're almost there.

Lorna Lea

Essence

I talk to you, you're always there.
You keep me sane with things unfair,
You tell me that I'm not alone,
You always listen when I moan.

I see a special side to you,
You let me know I'm someone too,
You never lie and always answer
You really are my life enhancer.

I am lost without your heart,
You know that we can never part,
You are my essence, keep me whole
You are me, you are my soul.

Alison Ryan

Life

A shove, a push it's such a rush
　　Life cannot go to waste.
Just make the most, see coast to coast
　　Do it with some haste.
When you wake up, say, 'Oh what luck,
　　Another day of pleasure,'
Make sure each day, love laugh and play
　　Life is here to treasure.

Every minute is time gone past,
　　So do yourself a favour,
Live each moment to the full
　　Enrich your life and savour.
Sleep each night with pleasant thoughts
　　These reach you in your dreams,
Be nice to someone every day,
　　For we're all human beings.

Carol Richmond

Don't Give Up The Fight

Life can be hard and sometimes cruel
There're times when the going can get tough
When everything seems to be against us
And sometimes we feel like we've had enough
We never know what life will throw at us
And sometimes life just ain't fair
Just when things are going smoothly
It has a habit of catching us unaware
You've just got to take the rough with the smooth
At the end of the tunnel there's always some light
And you never know what tomorrow will bring
So whatever you do, don't give up the fight

Stuart Jackson

Drop It!

I'm reminded of that wagging tail
Which clearly answered
My command of 'Drop it lad!'
With, 'No! I'm quite enjoying this.
I'll hold on though I know it's bad.'

Then again from puppy's lowered head
And ears so drooping,
Just as clear response I get:
'Well, yes, I know I'm really wrong
But shan't give in to you just yet!'

What reminded me of these two scenes?
'Twas Christ's commandings
And my own response of 'No'
When, 'Drop that train of thought,' he prompts.
Oh, why did I not let it go?

Far more patiently than I would chide,
My Saviour trains me.
'Help me, Saviour readily
To let Thee turn my mind around
From self-filled themes to thoughts of Thee.'

Praise, thanksgiving, prayer, forgiveness, love
Will guide my thinking
When I yield to His desires
And let Him cleanse, renew my mind
So that of Godless themes it tires.

Elma Heath

Healing Knowledge

Miracle Earth,
nurturing precious healing plants and trees,
I honour your bounteous beauty . . .

Thank you most powerful Creator,
for giving us your love and our ability to learn
the sumptuous secrets of curing seeds, berries, flower blossoms,
roots and leaves, to digest, inhale, and caress our skin.

Thank you for this miracle Earth,
meticulously positioned for our planned existence.
May we trust, love in return, appreciate and
strive for the safety of our space home.
To absorb and breathe in the healing knowledge and
breathe out on this wondrous planet paradise, a
universal boundless gratefulness . . .

Looking around, it's all here.
God has laid it at our feet, placed it before our eyes.
Our bodies can touch it.
Our senses are primed to perceive it.

Seek and see the healing knowledge.
Our powerful Creator has moved my pen,
one of many pens, to assist the Earth inhabitants.
I am just a cog in a marvellous mechanism of life on Earth.
Remember me, in the form of Carol Ann,
who tried her best to help and encourage the appreciation
of our miracle Earth, with this little piece of simple,
but purposeful writing.

Don't let the healing knowledge slip you by.
It's all here. It's all given. Just open your eyes to our
miracle Earth and joyously breathe it in and let it refresh
and pleasure you as we share our travel to eternity.

Carol Ann Darling

From My Lips That Kissed Thee

From my lips that kissed thee
I send a heartfelt plight,
Thro' the window, o'er the tallest tree,
Deep into the night,
Past the shadows, the brightest star,
Flying o'er the waning moon,
Whether you roam near or far
My words will seek you, find you soon,
Heed my voice as it calls for you
In a wistful, sighing song,
It searches for love pure and true;
Yours has been so all along,
'O loved one, come make my heart soar:
Bestow upon me your kiss once more!'

Sally Darby

Love

Love is encouragement and hope
given gentle voice, so words
become wings on which
our souls can fly.

And on this path I came upon
a clearing where I could rest
and gather scented memories
to remind me I was blessed,
for despite the hardship
of this, my lonesome trail
and the times I felt completely lost
in yet another gale,
love would always call to me,
come shelter from the storm,
so I could face the future
encouraged by new dawns,
and as I gaze around me now
at what lies up ahead,
an angel's beauty shines a light
on every step I tread.

Jean Caldwell

Spring's Awakening

The shafts of sunshine piercing through the hedge
cast streaks of lights upon the frosty road.
Across the hill, the trees and shrubs, like ghosts
creep upward through the shifting misty shroud.

The fields lie covered with a crust of snow,
just as though nature in anticipation,
had iced the meadows like a wedding cake,
so smooth and white, to greet spring's celebration.

Some lambs, who'd shivered through the colder days,
and sheltered close beneath their mother's shade,
find life within their spindly legs, to jump
with sheer delight along the frosty glade.

A lonely walker briskly steps his way,
pausing to breathe the air, so crystal-clear.
While high in the boughs, the chaffinch sings for joy,
his trilling notes proclaiming spring is near.

The hedgerows, drab and brown, lie dormant still,
but hiding 'neath the twigs, small buds await
the coming warmth, to burst them into life,
and spread a wreath of green from gate to gate -

showing, that from the bitter winter's gloom
is born again in spring, a season new.
Giving us hope to wake, and start afresh,
revived like plants by sun and sparkling dew.

Maureen Powell

Untitled

I trod the beech and pine-clad paths
    Listened to the rippling water say
This is a piece of Heaven
    God dropped to Earth one day
Mighty trees of beech towering above
    The glen, their graceful foliage
Making a lacy canopy
    And here and there the blue sky
Peeps through, while the sun
    Dapples the carpet of bluebells below
And tranquillity reigns over all.
    Banks of autumn leaves are
Huddled here and there, they will
    Feed the earth again as they
Decompose, a breeze wafts the smell
    Of wild garlic through the air and the
River gurgles its way down to meet the sea
    Lapping the boulders as it flows.
For this habitat of woodland things I give
    Thanks to the Creator of all things,
That He has blessed Ballaglass.

M S Hardman

It's A Good Life

As I awake, another morn
Stretch and yawn, breathe deep
Winter sun beams through the drapes
It's time to cast off sleep

Look from the window to frosty roofs
Sparkling white and clear
It's just so good to be alive
Watching the day appear

So many sounds in the morning air
Feathered friends arrive
Singing, whistling, squawking loud
In this garden of plenty they thrive

The colours of spring are all around
Bringing new life to the earth
Purple, yellow, white and pink
Nothing can better their worth

Wispy white clouds in a deep blue sky
Cool, clean air to breathe
It means so much just being here
It's not my time to leave

I sit by the fire, my dog by my side
Watching the flames burn bright
Peaceful thoughts fill my head
I'll sleep content tonight.

Esther Jones

When

When you are down but not quite out
When you wonder what life's about
You think that maybe it's passed you by
Breathe deep, give it another try
When you laugh, shrug off life's cares
Pick up, execute all life's dares
Meet every challenge expectantly
Overcome it with vitality
You won't be down, you won't be out
Because that's what life is all about.

Dora Watkins

Take Heart

The day was bright when we set out
Upon the mountain road.
The shining peak was beckoning,
Packed lunch our only load.

The first hour went quite smoothly,
Just a gentle upward slope.
We both were fresh and vigorous,
Our minds were full of hope.

The pace began to slacken
When the first few miles were spent.
Determined though, to reach our goal
We firmly onward went.

When gasping breath proclaimed that we
Had both begun to tire,
That peak seemed to be mocking us,
It surely had grown higher!

Temptation's voice said, 'Give up now,
You'll never climb so high.
Besides, there still are miles to go.
'Tis foolishness to try.'

But turning round we saw below
The long, long way we'd come.

When overwhelmed by life's demands,
Take heart! Count what you've done.

V E Godfrey

The Beauty Of Your Heart

Beauty of your heart
That shines through your eyes
Whispered in the clouds
Of a golden soul
That is surrounded only by the
Gentleness that is shown in
Every touch surrounding
Your loved ones
With the elegance of togetherness
The beauty of your heart.

Samantha Vaughan

I Travel In My Thoughts!

Within my own thoughts I travel both far and wide
Making visits to snow-capped mountains
That seem to reach the very heights of Heaven -
Still more wondrous as I walk in valleys deep,
Sounds of endless flowing waters fill my ears.

There is no place hidden on this planet Earth I haven't seen -
From country walks near to home, to mountains tall and free -
As far as desert plains, a place on Earth one ever seeks the value
Of fresh water that can bring a true comfort to the very living soul.

Time and time again I travel in my own thoughts
Always seeking for places new -
Ready to explore, ready to enjoy the wonders
That are waiting there.

R P Scannell

The Citizens' Charter

We are all equal, these following rights are ours,
no one is superior or inferior, inequality devours,
regardless of age, gender, race, colour or religion,
for every single father, mother, ,daughter and son,
I have the right to ask and need whatever I require,
to express my feelings, good or bad, as I desire,
to refuse any requests or demands I cannot meet,
to have my opinions respected, as others I greet,
to change my mind, maybe, without saying why,
to make mistakes and not be perfect, though I try,
to follow my own values and standards, unaccused,
to say 'no' to anything that violates my values,
I have the right to determine my own priorities,
to *not* be responsible for others' words or deeds,
to be protected by the law, to be safe, and to know,
when the law is unjust or misapplied, to say so,
to expect honesty from others, as they do from me,
to be angry at those I love, whoever they may be,
I have the absolute right to be uniquely myself,
to feel fear, and say so, regardless of wealth,
to say 'I don't know' to anything that I am not sure,
to *not* give excuses or reasons for my behaviour,
to make the right decisions based on my feelings,
to my own space and time, for personal dealing,
to be playful and frivolous, when I need to be,
to be as healthy, if not more, as those around me,
to be in a non-abusive environment, no one suffers,
to make friends and be comfortable around others,
the right to better myself, to change and grow,
to learn what I need, to know what I could know,
to have my needs and wants, to be respected,
to be treated with dignity and respect, as expected,

I have the right, as we all do, to be happy and free,
to be the best parent that I could possibly be,
to raise my children to respect others and the law,
and to keep them safe from harm, for me to adore.

Christopher Higgins

Another Day Tomorrow

Although life seems impossible today,
There's always another day tomorrow.
I often say that, just to get through life,
With its worries and mishaps and sorrow.

We all try to do as much as we can,
Times are busy with everyone I know.
Days full of hustle and bustle and strife,
What can one do, but to go with the flow?

But sometimes it's nice, just to put off chores,
There's always another day tomorrow.
To relax, and think of creative things,
Dream inwardly about some place to go.

To sit and study the cloud formations,
To see bright, colourful plants in a row.
To watch the birds; to see butterfly wings.
Oh! Doesn't nature put on a good show.

So I'll have to take the good with the bad,
Thank God for another day tomorrow.
Be happy, and do the best that I can,
Throughout my lifetime, be it high or low.

D Ranson

The Poppy Seed

A self sown seed, from whence it came I know not
But there it grew, from strength to strength went on.
Until it stood tall and full of blossom
Beauty rare, a joy to gaze upon!

One single seed but now with pods of promise
As hundreds more await their turn to grow
And will in time, as season follows season,
One day, somewhere, their hidden beauty show!

Blown by the wind they find their place of nurture.
Warm spring rain that softens hard cold earth,
And so as nature turns full cycle
Once more to see sweet blossoms come to birth!

So it is, we too can know the wonder
Of seed that grows within the heart of man.
Seed softly sown by wind of God's own Spirit
To draw us close, as is His wondrous plan!

The seed may lie for many years unheeded
Until the time conditions cause to stir,
And gentle rain of Holy Spirit nurture
Brings first shoots of love to occur!

Oh joy of joys when seed is activated,
First knowledge dawns; the secrets of New Birth!
All life is new and Heaven's way is opened
To share good news across the whole wide earth!

Then comes the time, strong growth and myriad blossoms
Abound, for all the world to share,
God's word goes forth again, full cycle,
More seed is sown, His Holy blossom rare!

E Bruce

The Welsh Marches, In Springtime

All around us, the reddened landscape sped past,
Intermingled by fresh green fields, sweetly renewed,
The live-giving rain, dripping, from heavens o'ercast.
A hidden sun sends golden warmth to earth, imbued
Upon the bright yellow, glowing joy of oil-seed rape,
So intensely that each needs to avert their gaze
To secretly scan lustrous fast-moving cloud-shapes,
Hovering, floating on by, to reveal a sudden solar blaze,
To cover th'awakening with well-being again.

The newly-planted soil already shows tender shoots,
Nurtured unfailingly by the Great Provider's hand.
And floriating goodness will emerge from scattered roots,
When God's tool, the farmer, tills his soil, as planned,
Allowing hedgerow dividers to remain in their place,
He hurriedly repairs the sweeping low stone walls,
Fringing aromatic pastures where wildflowers creep apace,
The hardworking man answers his Maker's calls
To wisely nourish the earth, as God's planner.

For St George's Day, profusions of bright dandelions glow,
Beneath early creamy-white hawthorns, laden with may.
And high crows' nests jostle large globules of mistletoe,
Too hard for us to reach and there they must stay!
But we can touch pink-tinged horse chestnut racemes,
As they point skywards and dance divinely in the trees,
Rejoicing in the overall warmth of the sun's beams,
Spreading o'er the marches, tinged by a chill breeze.
And, all around us, God's love surrounds.

Swift clouds crossing the sun cause shadows to speed by,
Illuminating the horizon in various lilac-blue shades.
Sedate riverside willows given an unearthly glow, are nigh,
Almond and cherry trees, whose sweet-smelling clusters pervade
The senses, and mating birds in heavily-hung wisteria dance

And call their song, as cowslips with daffodils shyly cling
Below the quickthorn's pristine white blossoms, which prance
With laburnum blooms and orange broom, as birds sing
An evening lullaby, in umbrous splendour.

Julia Eva Yeardye

Memories

Resting alone by the farmyard gate
She looked across the field at the still quiet lake,
Swans and ducks swimming gracefully by
Lifted her spirits and she remembered why
She came to this place with its memories dear,
Of rabbits, badgers, foxes and muntjac deer
Birds singing sweetly in the tall oak trees,
The gentle sound of humming of the bumblebees
She remembered the days long ago on the farm,
A beautiful place – unspoilt and calm
Now she is ready to leave this land,
Glad in the knowledge that it remains in God's hand.

Christine Hardemon

Anyone should know
Anyone with blind hate
Hasn't got a real case

Those who stand by, cannot see
Create pain for future scene

They seem to stick like superglue
But people tell me it isn't true
Their time will come, and out of the blue

All three will wish their time not now
Had spent their time on truth, they frown.

Geof Farrar

Awakening

After a long dark winter our senses take to wing,
Birds in the morning, how loudly they sing,
Splashing of yellow, daffodils rise,
Bees they awake flying out from their hive,
Primrose appears once again in the hedge,
Hatchlings try flying, their wings gently spread,
Pink sticky buds on the trees, they burst out,
The cuckoo is singing, his song he does shout,
The lambs gambol over the mountain with glee,
All fluffy and white, in delight, see them flee,
Cows in the meadow with new lush grass,
Munching and chomping - left out at last,
Calves suckle udders, the best of the milk,
With the sun on their backs, shining like silk,
We look for the swallows, the first one to spy,
A long arduous trip from South African skies,
Winter is over, the cycle has turned,
A long dark winter - new life has returned.

W Curran

Positivity Means Progress

The good days counterbalance
The ones when nothing goes right.
Life is always kinder to
Those of positive outlook,
Their ready smile, eagerness -
Willing to give it a go,
Coming up with the answers.
Their example directs us
To much greater fulfilment,
Turning Hell into Heaven.

Alexander Winter

Day By Day

Whatever the future you pursue,
No matter how rugged the climb,
You will get there, by trying your best
And taking one step at a time.

Forever is hard to imagine,
The *future* may seem far away,
But every new dawn, brings a wonderful chance,
To do what you can, *day by day.*

So my prayer today Lord Jesus,
This I am asking of *You,*
Give me strength for today,
Then show me what I must do.

Whatever the task, be it great or small,
Or the menial ones to fulfil,
May I know they are in *Your plan,*
And I'm carrying out *Your will.*

And to those I meet each day,
May they see *Your love* in me,
While carrying out Your daily plan
My happiness will see.

Yesterday has gone dear Jesus,
Tomorrow may never be mine,
Lord help me today, then show me the way,
To take *one day* at a time.

Will A Tilyard

Why?

Why do our best thoughts slowly creep
into our minds whilst others sleep?
What innovative flair has gone
whilst other bodies slumbered on?
With what inkling has our mind
left others far, so far, behind?
And yet when morning comes we wake,
our thoughts unbounded we forsake
and face the day as others do
and then forget it all – do you?

Robert Tose

23rd April

Saint George is our patron
We gladly proclaim
And on this his feast day
We honour his name.

A valiant soldier,
He fought the good fight
And died as a martyr
Defending the right.

Red cross on white background,
His flag, we will raise
And trust it is honoured
In England always.

May all of the nation
Find love brings true peace
And strive to express it
Until battles cease.

Harriet McCaul

Butterfly

Butterfly graceful with beauty serene
Pray tell me your purpose and what it should mean
That in God's house you choose to be passing your days
Oft times the substance of worshippers' gaze.
  Your world the nave, the chancel, and choir
  That we may but wonder, your presence inspire.

Butterfly silent with wings but a breath
Perchance the herald of those who in death –
Have slipped from this orb for they surely know
That peace in God's kingdom can chains overthrow.

Butterfly heedful in patient repose
Maybe our maker who cannot suppose –
That all of his children are faithful in turn
Since grace in creation some fail to discern.

Butterfly frail yet sustained in this place
Perhaps a mirror for our own mortal face
Born from beginnings with promise made sure
And transformed with brilliance, in God's love, secure.

Stephen Morley

Heartache

Now you can see that life won't last forever,
Close your eyes for a few minutes and think:
Didn't she love you above anything?
Weren't you, with her, happier than ever?

Now she's passed away and tears fall from your eyes,
Close your eyes and recall your memories.
Wasn't she the image of your fantasies?
Didn't you live where paradise lies?

Now you're alone 'cause your beloved departed,
Remember that your love still lives, enlightened
By the perfect memory you still keep.

Don't suffer in vain, for she's in Paradise!
Keep her image and, for her sake, arise!
Keep her alive showing your love's still deep!

Carla Sofia Lopes Ribeiro

Dawn

She comes awake,
oblivious,
around her, the world
is held in that breath-caught moment,
before her sunrise
reassures the day.
Chasing away
the cynical shadows of doubt,
where yesterday stumbled.

G H Roberts

Untitled

God gives us *help* in all we do
He *helps* us to learn our whole life through
Let's help others and show the way
To the people *in need* of our *help* each day
Let's make this a better world for our children
To share our whole life through
When my grandchildren come through the door,
It makes me smile for evermore
Just to see their *smiling faces*
Gives me a feeling no one replaces.

S Mathers

Happy

Yes, I am single but happy,
Happy as a sane person can be,
Because I'm deeply in love with you,
You know that you are in love with me.

Me, I have no doubts of your feelings,
Feelings, clear from looks you were stealing.
Stealing, from under heavy-browed eyes,
Eyes, conveying love without surprise.

S Mullinger

Sunshine

S unshine, nature's antidepressant
U niversal 'Prozac'
N ever fails to lift your spirits
S preading warmth across your skin
H ealing past injuries
I njecting warmth into your bones
N ew-found vitality
E nergising your whole body.

Christine Collins

Fragility Of Happiness

Once humans were a happy lot,
Born in the Garden of Eden,
But to sin, paradise was lost . . .
Degraded, as thro' flotation.

Is happiness a way of life?
Of human life: I that must stress!
Yet see how loaded stays the dice,
Cast on humankind's haplessness.

Animals - those wild beasts of prey . . .
Tame . . . domesticated as well,
They may have joy, but can one say
That in true happiness they dwell?

If closely looked at, and one finds
It's based upon some equation,
Or mainly for innocent minds
Till they reach the age of reason?

Some humans have found happiness,
In varied walks o' life they strode.
They kept unsoiled their innocence;
Or, regained thro' some pious mode.

But generations of them . . . those
Shorn of soul and reputation,
Have found it elusive to choose
Happiness within their station.

But happiness of ecstasy
Wrought by music and other arts,
Or love's own world of fantasy,
Spurs flights to soar and thrill all hearts.

Malcolm Henry James

As A Voice... Crying In The Wilderness

We do not know the hour
Or the minute that is true
When with the twinkling of an eye
Our world is torn in two

From sunshine into showers long
From daytime into night
A hand that turns the light switch off
We're blind without our sight

And 'Jesus wept' the Bible says
So we are not alone
When sitting in a darkened room
Just thinking on our own

There has to be a reason why
God made these tears to cry
As well as smiles to greet the day
And when you leave . . . 'a sigh'

To see the 'rainbows' through our tears
It gives us hope I know
Or sunbeams on a cloudy day
Through eyes so red to show

That tears when shed emotionally
It shows a 'heart' that's crushed
In pieces like a jigsaw now
From lips that too are hushed.

But tears they are a symbol too
Of joy when meeting those
Who come back home into your life
A blooming summer rose

And tears of happiness as well
At wedding there have been
A baby's birth, a late-night kiss
Engagement, 'yes' . . . I've seen

To cry with laughter is so grand
With arms around your friends
Or cry for those who went away
'I love you' . . . message ends

Yes crying is a way that we
Without a word that's said
Will show our love from you to me
From soul, not from our head

A bittersweet reminder then
That tears can always be
Through eyes, red with tear stains now
Just love . . . 'compassionately'

Robert Eric Weedall

Thank You Lord

My dear Lord, what words convey
The way You fill my life each day.
When times are hard and I feel down,
You are always there, always around.

When I am happy and feeling gay,
There You are to share my day.
I'm so lucky to have a friend,
Who is with me now, and at the end.

Sandra Wylie

An Outstanding World

The sun rises in the morning and shines all over our land,
It makes people happy and roll around in the sand,
As the night-time grows closer and the sun has to set,
It's then that the moon and stars will be met.

The clouds are like big silky pillows of wool,
If only we could feel them, that would be cool!
They make all sorts of shapes in that beautiful sky,
And even at night it's there that they lie.

The man on the moon holds such a proud face,
As he keeps a close watch over this wonderful place.
He glows so brightly so everyone can see,
What a peaceful and beautiful world this can be.

The stars in the sky they shine oh so bright,
Without a shadow of a doubt they will appear every night,
You stand and you gaze and maybe even say hello,
And sometimes you wonder what they see below.

The world is an oyster for every man to use,
With all its great nature you may sometimes win or lose,
One thing is for certain that when God created this place,
He made it for one hell of an outstanding human race.

John Fullerton

Sunrise

A new day is beginning.
All the birds are singing.
First rays of light sweep the land,
Coming in from the east,
Moving over sea and sand.

Go to your window,
Feel the warmth upon your face.
No more is the cold night air,
It has gone without a trace.

Seeing the sunrise is beautiful,
A wonderful start for the day,
Something you wouldn't want to miss out on,
Or have, any other way.

A new day is beginning,
All the dark clouds are thinning.
First rays of light gently sweep the land,
As if being brushed by the Creator's hand.

Stand in the dawn air
To feel the warmth upon your skin,
The night has passed you on by,
And now the day begins.

Seeing the sunrise is wonderful,
A beautiful start for the day,
So don't you miss out on it,
Or settle for another way.

Kevin Welch

A Tiny Baby

(To my mum and dad)

A tiny baby cries in turning space,
And watches Earth, learning its easy pace:
A guardian angel she spies, then giggles
With fingers and toes, then points and wiggles:

Is there an angel resting by my side
Or perched as a parrot, wings out wide?
On shoulders, ancient, mine, I carry her,
And like a kitten, I hear the angel purr:

So does our God, a tickling stick possess
To tickle ribs or toes, any recess?
He has a sense of fun, I have no doubt
But look, when the Devil wins, does He pout?

Now my guardian angel swings along,
And whistles tunes among the happy throng:
In cool of evening she sits on my bed,
And keeps away monsters, the evil dead:

As morning sky, now clears, she watches,
The 'city just' rises, yawning loud, washes:
I thank the Lord, in simple prayer soft,
For guardian angels now gone aloft:

O' blue, the seas are burning fields of love,
And red the blood is falling from above:
A rook is crying under arches of cloud:
A prayer goes and God is highly proud.

Edmund Saint George Mooney

Daily Reflections

God's Daily Blessing

My oh my, thank God each day
For each day's a blessing, come what may
Whether raining or sunny, good day or bad
A blessing from God you will have had
So thank and praise Him each time you pray
For the blessing He's given you, of another day.

Royston Davies

A Roller Coaster Ride

Life may be a roller coaster ride
But it doesn't mean you have to hide.
There may be many ups and downs.
Happy times, sad times, smiles and frowns
But you shouldn't let evil get in the way.
You should look forward to each day.
Don't let all of it trouble you.
Get on with life and things you do.
Don't let life pass you by
You'll regret it when you die.
Looking back on what you did
Times when you were depressed and hid.
Take life in your stride
Enjoy your own roller coaster ride.
You never know when happiness is near
Or depressing times bringing fear.
Don't dwell on all that is bad
And miss out on things you should have had.
Celebrate good, grow in strength
Live your life to a reasonable length.
Take risks, try something new
Do things just for you.
Look to the future, don't dwell on the past.
Enjoy the present while it lasts!

Kirsty Lane (14)

Daily Reflections

You And Now

If you can look at this
you can see.
If you can hear it read
you can listen.
Understand - or disagree -
you can think and feel.
You are you
and you are now.

Grieve for those you've lost -
it shows you've loved.
Keep them living
when you think:
not old, or ill, or terrified.
And as for the gaps,
what we can't have -

everything is in your head:
more ideas than the stars in the sky
the grains in the sand
the crystals in the glacier.
You can withstand pain and fear.
Remember, your mind is free.
Only you can be you
and you are now.

A E Evans

Pointing The Way

As you walk through the countryside,
footpath signs point the way to your destination.
Bees gently land on the wild flowers,
collecting the nectar to feed their young.
Birds dart in and out of the hedgerows,
finding food to take back to their nests,
to feed their fledglings.
Cows munch contentedly on the fresh spring grass,
murmuring to each other in low tones,
busily swishing their tails to disperse the insects annoying them.
Sheep are settling down to rest after eating their fill.
The trees are gently moving their branches in a light breeze.
The blue sky, vacant of any cloud, creates a wonderful backdrop
with the sunshine illuminating the coloured landscape.
God created this wealth for us to enjoy.
Jesus points the way for us to follow in His footsteps.
Walk the way of life with Him.

Linda Knight

The Horizon

The days move on
And time has gone
That puts space
Between you and me.

And I must tread
This long, long road
That fate has deemed
My life should be.

I watch the child
That has your face
Leap forward and embrace
Each day with joy.

Young heart and bones
That has no fear
And reaches out with
Everything that I hold dear.

It's then I know
What God has planned
For everyone upon
These lands.

That nothing happens
Quite by chance
He knows! And gives us compensation
In things that make our lives enhanced.

And I know you are there
Just beyond the far horizon
As you always said you'd be
Waiting for me.

Joan May Wills

Angel Without Wings

Last night I asked God a question
During my bedtime prayer
I asked Him when He sends for me
Could I be an angel up there?

He told me, 'When the time is right
I will send for you'
He said, 'You have years and years to go
And lots of work to do'

He said I was very thoughtful
And very caring too
'But just for now keep doing
What you're down on Earth to do'

He told me to be happy
And do lots of happy things
He said, 'You are an angel down there
An angel without wings.'

Helen Louisa Gray

Solace

(For a bereaved friend)

I have a whirlpool of emotions
Swirling across my being
The pain and anger I accept
Not to play down what has happened
Nor to write it off completely
But to allow the fear to be driven away
So that the sorrow may stay
For while fear impoverishes.
Sorrow enriches.

(So) even as countless questions assail my mind,
And bitterness threatens to stifle me,
I take a deep breath,
Allow my renewing
And pray to be made whole again
The light is not yet dim
The comforter is not far away
Peace is my portion.

Seyram Ama Avle

Quiet Quad

Dreamy drifts of downy daises
Star the sunny quad,
Delightful fair and flowery faces
Lifting up their thanks to God,
By just being daisies . . .

'Blossom where you've planted,'
Now that is good advice
Don't think if only, only,
I was someone really nice . . .
God made you special . . . be yourself.

Musing on the way we worry,
The hectic lives we lead;
Has He not promised to provide
Us with everything we need?
So let's be thankful . . .

We may not get all we want . . .
It wouldn't be wise you know!
But we have so many blessings,
So like those flowers that grow
Let's gratefully lift our heads . . . (to Him).

Thank You Father, for the daisies
Pure and white as driven snow,
Reminding us we should stop striving,
Trust in You to make us grow,
For we're Your children . . .

Dorothy Yeates

Dawn Chorus

Today will be a good day
happen what might;
Love and truth, the way

Nor shall grief hold sway
over the longest night;
today will be a good day

Let loneliness find its way
into Heaven's light;
Love and truth, the way

Though a sandman say
we stay out of sight,
today will be a good day

As written in God's clay,
know wrong from right,
love and truth, the way

Pain, guilt, our Calvary
as Earth's ills we fight;
Today will be a good day,
love and truth, the way.

R N Taber

Angels Calling

When you feel a gentle breeze
pass your cheeks.
Then you have been given an
angel's kiss.
With this special blessing your
angels will guide you and be with
you always.

Tracey Anson

My People

I have set before all race and creed an ever open door
But man is wilful, walks away, his heart is closed once more.
Enticed by worldly pleasure, a love affair with sin
Already lost in battle, impossible to win.
He does not see the plight of those in poverty and need
His driving force is selfishness, avarice and greed
But the door of life stands open, propped open by a cross
If but one man returns to me I shall not count it loss.
For my ways are higher, fairer, and to know them is to gain
True liberty and freedom, then peace on Earth shall reign.

Carol Awdas

God's Power In Your Weakness

God loves to use us though we're weak
We need Him every hour.
He let it happen so that He
Could demonstrate His power.

If He used 'perfect' folk His work
On Earth would not get done.
He chose to package up His power
In an unlikely one.

It's when we're weak that we are strong,
God's promises are true.
He says, 'I'm with you all the way,
I'm making you brand new.'

God knows what's best and so He hides
His power in simple things.
He wants us to depend on Him,
It's daily strength He brings.

Your most effective ministry,
Will come out of your pain,
The things you found so hard to share,
Will bring to others gain.

So when you think, 'God won't use me
So fragile, flawed and weak.'
Remember you're that small clay pot,
But God's power at its peak!

Gillian Humphries

Modern Age

Early next year I'll be eighty-three,
and still as busy as can be.
Oft-times I wonder how I found,
time to work or till the ground.
I still delve into sharps and flats,
my clavinova sees to that.
The PC helps me keep in touch,
with friends and loved ones missed so much.
At the potter's art I try my hand,
the things I make, friends think are grand.
My scooter is fine to get around,
saves on petrol many a pound.
With my nose stuck into a book,
often I forget it's time to cook.
The day is too short to fit all in,
I strive to protract it but never win.
One still enjoys a friendly chat,
when 'seniors' speak of this and that.
Then it's time to think of bed,
to take my rest after prayers are said.
So for you, dear reader, what will life be,
when *you* reach the age of eighty-three?

Ken Blomley

We Are All The Same

We are all the same
And we are all different
For I am, at the same time,
Both weak and strong
Skilled and clumsy
Afraid and brave.

Helper and helped
I am provider and I am needy.
I am loser and winner
My success and my failure are two sides of the same coin.

What is important, Lord?
To try; to do my best; to never give up;
To see the world from the opposite viewpoint;
To walk in someone else's experience.

When we see we are all the same
And when we see we are all different
Then we can live together in peace.
Amen

Maria Dabrowska

Daily Reflections

Forever Nowhere

Deep in the kingdom of Nowhere,
Where some day and one day are found,
Where maybes and what ifs are wondered,
And all possibilities abound,
This is where hope has more value,
Than objects could ever withhold,
Where dreams and the dreamers are welcomed,
And no dream is ever too bold,
For this is the land of Forever,
Forever for any to find,
Open to any who wish it,
And to any who open their mind.

Sara Rhys

A Smile

A smile is what the world loves to see
It creates a warm bond from you to me
A smile opens doors and one's heart
It reduces anguish when one has to part.

A smile is encouragement one always needs
A reward and thank you for good deeds
A smile is a lovely opening gambit
Welcoming you into one's personal ambit.

A smile can dispel one's gloom
Brings joy back and banish doom
A smile will come when you are well and happy
Help to cheer those sad and snappy.

A smile brings back the verve to be alive
Tells misery to be gone and take a dive
A smile can be a thank you - an expression
It can send a most positive indication.

A smile can flow from everyone on Earth
It's in us to maturity from birth
Wouldn't it be wonderful if we all smiled many times a day
Making living for all, one long, happy holiday.

Terry Godwin

Your Face

Sunny days replace the haze
Life is fun and calm
The moon is soft, her face is bright
Protecting stars from harm.
Flowers lift their heads to smile
Cuddled in the breeze
Leaves that rustle in the night
Are coats for precious trees
And all around in nature's web
Life is fresh and new
And happiness is offered free
I love it all, don't you?
So spare a thought for hidden gems
The air, the warmth, the space
And live your life best you can
With love upon your face.

Yvonne Stafford

Who Makes The Rules?

The steamroller of life goes trundling on,
Crushing hopes we've held so long,
Who makes the rules, who decides?
Who controls the turning tides?

They say that self-determination
Is the essence of our nation,
There's nothing that you can't achieve
If you have courage and believe.

When dealing with life's vicissitude
Don't let self-doubt and fear intrude,
Stand firm, stand tall, hold your ground
Don't let misfortune grind you down.

If your self-belief is strong
Protect yourself and soldier on,
Counsel yourself, change your view
It's your perception that makes it true.

Reserves of strength you need to find,
Body controlled by strength of mind,
Focus on your inner self
Nurture your spirit and safeguard health.

Self-reliance is the key
To being what you want to be,
Don't let others make the choice
Speak out loudly, use your voice.

Life's not always as it seems
There's still a place for those with dreams
Who makes the rules, whose decision?
You, yourself, your own volition.

Kay Seeley

Today

*(Yesterday is gone, tomorrow never comes
what lies between the two can only be today)*

Today is only a short time, given to us to enjoy
Take each and every day as it comes
And be truly thankful it has been given to you
Never take any part of your life for granted
Help all those who are unable to help themselves
And then at night when you lie down to rest
You can truly say you have done your best
And in the morning when you awake
So much is given for your sake,
Your most precious gift is another day
To enjoy with others in your own
Special way.

Brian Hill

End Of Holiday

The final curtain falls -
departure comes.

Pack up disconsolately,
vacate homely room.

With heavy heart
say goodbyes
to kind folk.
Nevermore to be encountered.

Train ebbing slowly -
Goodbye.

Arrive in London.

On seeing familiar bustle,
pangs of sadness vanish,
to be replaced
by warm feelings of gladness
on returning.

And home again,
refreshed and well.

Remember nice people,
happy fellowship enjoyed,
sights and experiences
shared and loved
together.

Recount to family and friends
the joy of beach and country,
all you saw, heard and felt.

Left with happy memory,
enriched by friendly folk.

Alison Lingwood

The Real Wonders Of The World

The truth of love,
The lies of hate,
The wings of beauty,
The secret of fate.

The shadows of evil,
The clouds of despair,
The temptations of desire,
The kindness of care.

The breath of an angel,
The flames of the fire,
The faith of a spirit,
The mind of a liar.

The scent of the flower,
The lock without a key, but,
The love of a family
Is the most important to me.

Lisa Kyle (13)

Jewels Of Life

Hello my dear friend, I know that you're sad,
I've been there too and it's hard to be glad,
When your partner and loved one, has long gone away,
And you miss and you grieve for him every day.
But you have to remember that we'll never know,
If they are happy or sad wherever they go,
They can't come and tell us, so we have to believe,
That some greater power decides when they leave.
Removes all their suffering and eases their pain,
Renews their spirit to be born again.
Destiny's blessings like children on loan,
Their spirits were searching to find their right home.
Then they stayed with us, loved with us, and made us smile,
And many times said, I'll be back in a while.
So take of my friendship, while we two remain,
Give thanks for the sunshine, the snow and the rain,
The breezes and bird songs, the hills and the trees,
The scent of the roses, the buzzing of bees.
That we wake every morning to a new precious day,
The blue of a summer sky the smell of the hay.
The colours of rainbows, the greetings of friends.
For the extra time here, the rules that are bent,
To let us stay longer, than the time we've been lent.
Good night my dear friend, may your sleep time be sweet
In dreams kiss your loved one, and tomorrow we'll meet.

Jean Jones

My Dear Sweet Mother

Now that you have become older,
But, not so grey,
You have suffered a severe stroke,
That has rendered you disabled.
Yet, your spirit is always high,
And, your heart is always warm.
You tell me stories, about how it used to be,
And, the things you used to get up to.
I see you in a new light now,
You are a little girl once again.
Your eyes light up,
As you tell of your antics.
Ones that I had never dreamt of,
Or, even thought of.
Each morning, you tell a story.
You also tell me,
This is, so you will know me.
Who I am,
And where I come from.
My dear sweet mother,
You never cease to amaze me!

Violet Rustean

God's Will (And Testament)

From my domicile the heavens
I'm bequeathing all my wealth
I declare this my last testament
And leave you to yourselves.
In the presence of myself, I
Leave eternity to kill
And proclaim this to be God's will

The whole world is your relation
Please refrain from causing harm
Try to give without a motive,
Speak the truth and remain calm
Intermingle with the wise
And see you wish nobody ill
But if you're lost, then read God's will

May your favoured gains be wisdom,
Always strive for helpful change
Tolerate all difference
Realise you're not the same
Everything you do has consequence
And time does not stand still
So please take care . . . this is God's will
So please take care . . . this is God's will.

Ellis Creez

Heaven On Earth

Blue skies upon green fields,
Pink blossom on the ground.
Everywhere I look,
Heaven waiting to be found.
Birds lost in song,
As they take their gracious flight.
Their voices only silenced,
By the darkness of the night.
Next time you crave paradise,
Just step outside your door.
Heaven is here for everyone,
To enjoy and to explore.

Simon Raymond McCreedy

Don't Buy One - It's Free

(Dedicated to my grandchildren
who have shared these thoughts with me)

Learn to listen to the wind in the trees
and walk with nature a while.
Admire the sight of a hedgerow flower,
see the swallow nest under a tile.

Take a deep breath in a garden in bloom
with lavender, roses, sweet peas
and think that it costs you nothing at all
to enjoy such pleasures as these.

Show a small child the joys to be found,
in ladybird, butterfly, bee
and that little robin who'll come to your hand;
the apples glowing red on the tree.

In winter the frost sprinkles sparkle like jewels
and footprints may be made in fresh snow
and in autumn the blackberries offer a feast
if you find the place where they grow.

Peace and tranquillity often we lack
as we race around in our cars
yet, just out of sight, if we care but to search,
so much beauty and joy can be ours.

So, just for an hour or two, shrug off your cares,
leave the hot, hasty mainstream behind.
Peep round that corner, it's still waiting there
those things that bring joy to your mind.

Brenda Heath

Now That I Am Growing Old

I rest in comfort in my chair, now I'm growing old
And seek the album in my mind, its pages to unfold.
To look upon the pictures, as the scenes begin to flow
Which capture all the memories, of days so long ago.

From the early days of life, when young and just a child
When life was full of fun and games, and dreams could just run wild.
Then through days of adult life, with romance along the way
Careers and business learning, to finance you through your day.

I stood beside life's flagpole, where I saw its flag unfurled
Bringing scenes of natural beauty, in our lovely world.
The trees, the flowers, singing birds, and all the meadow green
Deserts and the golden sands, rivers and each rippling stream.

I see now family pictures, from golden days gone by
Now I feel a little moisture, on the cheek beneath my eye.
Just a tear of satisfaction, from the glorious memories there
As I turn the album's pages, in the comfort of my chair.

To those of you who are not old, there is no need to fear
For age will bring contentment, with the passing of each year.
Restful and more peaceful, you will find more time to spare
To turn your album's pages, in the comfort of your chair.

Donald Futer
(Bard of Bardney)

Passage

Emmanuel. 'God with us'. God with us all the time!
'God with us' through this winter, cold and long.
Christmas. His incarnation in all our trivial days.
Finished, the gifts and glitter. Ordinary life!

But Jesus (in His goodness) awaits the spring with us.
He's not above being buried in the patient earth.
He passes through His passion, inviting us to share,
To eat with Him the bread of boredom, suffering, tears,
Enduring such long waiting . . . (we thank you, Lord, so close).

And then – He springs to life, He's won, He's risen, now!
Won *our* resurrection, brought the world to birth.
Green and blossom flourish, hope can reign again,
Light shines through the tunnel, now we may rejoice!
We are the Easter people! Break into shouts of joy!
Glory to You, great Jesus, King of the spring. All hail!

Katharine Holmstrom

Note Of The Day

Flight of the butterfly,
An aria of perpetual beauty,
Birds soaring in the clouds
Doing acrobats in perfect time,
Like a ballerina's graceful line,
Or swans serene and proud.

Elephants trampling across the land,
Like a jungle drum,
Monkeys hanging by tails,
Swinging together in time,
Donkeys following in line,
Clip-clop plodding never fails.

We humans forget we have a choice,
To speak out in clear voice,
To keep God's creatures alive,
Help the Earth, then they survive.

E M Gough

An Early Morning Walk

Shrouded in mist the day dawns:
White vapour rises and melts
In the morning sun.
Dappled light breaks through leaf and branch
Playing with light and shade:
A new day is begun.

Rays from the day star dry away
Nightly fear and misty tear;
And opens wide its solar eye
To watch as dawn breaks into
Bright and glorious day:
Revealed in clear blue sky.

Across the path a blackbird runs:
Tears drop from overhanging branch:
A few leaves fall:
And silence shouts. Its deafening roar
Unheard by ears is felt by soul:
And peace rules over all.

Such sound was heard once long ago,
As God with Adam walked
In Eden's primeval bliss.
In creation's garden dwelt peace and love,
As God graced His newborn Earth
With heavenly kiss.

Seek out the early hours of dawn;
Before all earthly noise begins
Watch; wait; listen and pray.
Nature alone knows its creator's plan,
It seeks and finds a paradise
In each new day.

Ann Davies

My Dearest One

Thank you for all the wonderful years
That we have shared together,
And for all the wonderful years
I pray are yet to come.

Thank you for always being there
Whenever I've needed you,
And especially for being there
When I didn't know I needed you.

Thank you for all the happy times,
The tears and laughter we've shared,
For gently easing the sad times,
Holding me up when I was down.

Thank you for being my best friend,
My teacher and my lover.
Most of all I want to say thank you
For simply being you.

Polly Davies

Summer Sun

Winter's over! Now the warming sun
tells that summer has begun.
Listen to the buzz of bees,
and note the blossom on the trees.
See the busy, scurrying ant -
hear the birds' soaring descant.
Watch as they fly from here to there
to nests in trees, no longer bare.

Then watch their young, in maiden flight
in mornings that grow early, light.

See how the plants begin to grow -
and those weeds, too! Just row on row!
When latent buds burst forth in bloom
then scattered is the winter's gloom.
A sound of mower taming lawn -
in fields the sheep just lately shorn.
To watch a foal's exuberant chase
around the field in frenzied race.

The soft-eyed calf just newly born -
the sprouting of the summer corn.

The tumbling waters of the stream
released from bondage, swirling cream
and frothy-white round jagged rocks -
the sight of seabirds, numerous flocks
who squawk and quarrel, and then surge
forward on each sandy verge.
For once more the year has spun
and brought with it the summer's sun!

J Wildon

What Colour Today?

(Dedicated to a mother that I loved and lost)

If this day was a colour
    this day is blue,
It's the day we both sat
    the day we both knew.

If this day was a colour
    this day is black,
It's the day that you went
    never to come back.

If this day was a colour
    this day is purple,
It's the day you were dressed up
    ready for the funeral.

If this day was a colour
    there would be a rainbow today,
It's the day you are leaving
    there's no reason to stay.

If this day was a colour
    this day is white,
It's the day you reach Heaven
    with everything right.

Dianne Audrey Daniels

The Sun Will Shine Again

When you lose someone very dear to you
And life seems all in vain
When out of your world goes someone near to you
And there are no rainbows, only rain
When the night seems long and the day won't dawn
And laughing people seem insane
Hold on to that hope when there is nothing left to hope for
And the sun will shine again.

When all that remains is a face that seems blurred
And words repeating ever in your brain
And you can't quite face reality
And every road you take is 'memory lane'
When your world falls apart and the pieces don't fit
And two people close together cause you pain
Reach out beyond this timeless hour
Have the faith of the flowers in the rain
Though they've taken your dreams
And forsaken your schemes
And the lilies of the field are scarlet-stained
There is a world far beyond the horizon
Where no one waits in vain
Through the long lonely night
As you pray for the light
The sun will shine again.

Albert Edward Reed

Killing Me Softly

Snowflake
falling musically
from the sky,
like a scene
from an old movie,
are you as pure
as you appear
I wonder?

Does your hushed whisper
as I crush you
speak of silence
or release?
From where
did you come,
where were you formed?
And as you die

why can you offer me
nothing more than a sigh?

Russell Sparkes

Unconventional Nature

All nature has a ragged symmetry,
Ne'er planting seed in trim and tidy style:
There is pleasure in her loose disorder,
Unevenness in all things to beguile.
Nature's chariot
The wind, tarries not,

Pillowing, billowing white sails on sea
Hither and thither to blow men abroad;
Mixing and mingling skin colours and creeds,
Spilling the life seed of man in accord;
Rippling reflections
Sweet imperfections.

Birds blown above oceans swift, wing their way;
Beast roam wilderness in calm disorder,
Hedgerow and field full flush with wild flowers
Randomly sown, not tight like a hoarder.
Nature designs bold
Spreads uncontrolled.

Woodland growth shows rugged pattern'd splendour
Mixed in its canopy of dappled light,
Boasting myriad leaf shapes, one artist's hand,
In random art, our eyes perceive delight.
Man may endeavour,
Perfection never.

Pity those devoid of free sensation;
Time spins, then weaves magic webs to wrangle,
No silver thread to follow as we go,
Weft and warp of nature is a tangle,
Aim intentional,
Unconventional.

Doreen Roberts

Daily Reflections

Dreaming

Sitting all alone and dreaming,
Dreaming dreams of what used to be
Still they return ever appealing
Pleasurable treasures just for me
Visualising though my sight grows weaker
Your lovely face and all about you is divine
We had the most wondrous partnership
Together we were thought of as sublime
Alas you now are gone
And sadly I am left behind

When younger, oh, how we romanced!
Enjoyed every minute of each other's company
You so delightful and delicate
Like a soft bird on the wing
In those melancholy occasions you drove
All sadness away, I heard you sing
Driving away those fears you brought gladness
This to lighten my heart and life
You being such an adorable creature
It was decided that we should be husband and wife

Oh! Alas your reign did not linger
Struck down by Heaven's mighty force
For duties elsewhere you were required
You obeyed that might truly endorsed
Sadness then brought about my ill health
As calmly waiting day by day
For your assistance to improve my happiness
Unfortunately you never came my way
Of a brighter dawn that hails tomorrow
Of a greater future thus only you inspire
As I linger here dreaming continually
Your eternity's future was never ever denied.

R D Hiscoke

Alone Together

With open arms and closed eyes I feel you near.
Yet surrounded by my own demise I see you so clear.
You lift me up with a single touch of your spirit.
For in the darkest of nights I see your light forever lit.
I feel my mind take me up and away
As I watch my body on the ground to stay.

Nothing matters as up I glide.
Whispers in my ear as spirits confide.
Here I am, yet it really doesn't matter.
Lives, living, from my mind they just scatter.
Nothing but open thoughts slowly appear.
Here I am so far away and yet so near.

You make me feel so alive and free.
A mere touch is all that matters to me.
I feel so alive, so above this Earth.
I feel guilty, is this love deserved?
Yes, this love is mine, to me it is true.
On wings of love I will return to you.

Thomas Titchener

Not Alone

If at times you feel alone,
Please try not to despair,
Because someone's life wouldn't be as great
If you were not there.

I know that you don't realise,
But there's some things that you say,
That make me smile when I'm down,
And the darkness goes away.

They were talking about you yesterday,
Nothing but praise, I swear,
They would be lost without you,
I wish you could know how much we care.

I know sometimes you sit and cry,
I know sometimes you live in fear,
But my fears would have killed me by now
If you had not been here.

I know that words can be cheap,
But I do owe my life to you,
I hope you realise you're never alone,
Not whilst I am loving you.

J L Thomas

Changing Places

We all at some time wish for a different life
Many of us grumble and complain along the way
We foolishly reflect on how things might have been
And curse our misfortunes that sometimes end our dreams
We curse our bad luck at missing the last bus
While some younger lives are taken and not by their choice
Still we waste our energies and so often our voice
Stop plaguing your mind with negative attitudes
Breathe life into your old frame, life hates solitude
Many younger lives would love to grow old
Many younger lives would love to be a parent and
Have the chance to scold
As long as they could pass on the beauty learned and untold
Never let life go
It's there for us all to sow
Forget your airs and graces
There are many who would change places
To be given your chances
At life and all its dances
Don't begrudge your pain and sorrow
If you know you have the chance of seeing tomorrow.

Mike Hynde

Prayer For The Day

Great God and Creator
Grant Your healing power
Upon body - mind - and soul
For time and burden have taken their toll
Let passing cloud and running stream
Be the source of peace and energy
Let gentle breeze and nodding flower
Be the inspiration of my inner peace
Let Your message come by whispering grass
And laughter by the sound of leaves
Hope in birdsong and rising sun
Fulfilment in setting sun
       And a job well done.

Clive Cornwall

A Lucky Year

Another year is under way
With hopes and aspirations too.
As we target new goals we aim to reach
That will benefit me and you.

If we are lucky enough to hold a job
Let us give it all we can.
And remember those unlucky ones
Whose luck unlike ours, ran

Should we have a family,
May they hold us in respect
For the way we give ourselves to them
And never do neglect.

Maybe we follow a belief
That God will help us through.
What's more He will watch over us,
In everything we do.

Gordon Barnett

Please Be Strong

Please think of me now I am gone,
Think of me and please be strong,
Remember the good things in the past,
Remember the love that always lasts,
Think of our children growing strong,
Forget all the bad things that went wrong,
Think of the love they are giving now,
Remember how we showed them how,
Think of me now I am gone,
Remember me and please be strong.

Ellen Gigg

Weakest Times And Moments Are When You're At Your Strongest

Jeannie love, don't be sad,
Bathe yourself in the experiences
God has blessed you with to
Strengthen your mind, body and soul.

Rejoice in your mistakes, because they are your blessings.
For you have been saved from yourself, by yourself.
Be with yourself for a while,
Learn the lessons sent to you,
Pave them out to take you to
Your destination in your life on Earth.

Jean Yvonne Thompson

Raindrops Down A Pergola

Raindrops down a pergola;
After all the rain;
Along its whole parameter;
Every one the same,
Glowing pearls all clinging round,
A pretty lady's breast;
Knowing she is so profound:
Wearing all her best,

Hanging there with equity,
Each the other's kin;
Though the rain has gone away,
Every curving vine;
Some are opal - some are pearl,
Some are onyx grey,
Some are like a turtle shell
A beach that's far away;

Gone the rain they quickly lend,
Amber blue and green,
As the sun's rays softly bend,
Diamonds through a screen,
Glistening raindrops end to end,
After all the storm,
All these colours as I stare,
The rainbow's lovely form;

Causing me to wonder why,
Something so per se;
God's unseen qualities testify,
In such a simple way . . .

Tom Ritchie

Thank You

Thank You for the morning
On waking up to hear
The song of birds singing
Of joy which is so clear

Thank You for the food
Upon the table stands
Various kinds of tasty things
From many different lands

Thank You for the folks
Who come and pass my way
With a kindly word or two
Makes the pleasure of the day

Thank You for the stars
That twinkle in the sky
For when I look to Heaven
I know You are standing by.

Joyce Gale

As We Now Part

As we now part heavy in silence and cascading tears
Each half broken-hearted to sever for years
Cold, pale is thy cheek as my lips brush to kiss
Truly, that hour foretold an ending like this

The dew of that morning felt chill on my brow
A stark siren warning that I still feel now
Forever shall I love thee, too deeply to tell
In a miasmic black hole I tripped and I fell

In secret we met
In silence now grieve
That our hearts would'st forget
A payment for my wrong deceit
Then how shall I greet thee
When our souls and our fears
As we die and thence rise
Hopefully together in silence and not tears.

Michael Boase

The Ultimate

Flying high,
Like a bird in the sky,
It's the closest I'll get to the stars.

Above the clouds,
The words spoken loud, 'You will never make it.'

My feet on the ground,
But what I have found,
I'm reaching for my dreams.

Do wishes come true?
Well I'm telling you,
Soaring for The Ultimate.

Melanie May

Bowl Of Life

Gaze into the bowl of life
where spheres of prismed light,
reflect upon the rings turning
Nature's candle burning.
Let the vision show you a way
where strength and peace shine to stay,
embrace the Earth and etheric rays
to clear away the hazy days.
Like swirling orange sunset sky
with golden ripples soaring high,
o'er emerald valleys rolling,
listen to the music calling.
Filaments in the hand to weave
Nature's gift, you believe,
like an arrow arcs the air
in the direction you see fair.
Find the staff that shines and guides,
touch the centre of Life, arise.

Sharon Townsend

Spring's Glory

What wonderful days in the country
now that the blossom is here!

From tightly curled balls
to fine frothy fronds –
such colours and shapes we see there!

From jewel-bright rose on bracken stem
and party-pink with green,
to the heaviest clotted-cream bunches
the hedgerows yet have seen.

Cherry blossom white and apple pink
and the subtle shades between
can lift the heart 'neath a grey-day sky
with their backdrop of vibrant bright green.

It stays but a moment, the blossom,
a short life, yet fine, and so sweet,
then on to the next blooms of spring-summer's scene
that nature lays out at our feet.

We stoop to the scent of the flower,
its humility thus do we share,
but the boughs of the blossom gaze heavenwards,
and the soul of humanity's there.

Maureen Horne

New Day

Take each day as if it were your last
See the sun's colours reflecting through the glass
Look into your heart and know you're alive
Start the day with a smile and you can only thrive

See the sky and all the birds' flight
See the trees and the shapely delight
Feel the grass between your toes
Sense the Earth and the wisdom it knows

Open your eyes to everything that's there
Look beyond the forms and see all the care
Know that God must have skill beyond words
To create such wonder for us to observe.

Ricky N Lock

Bereavement

When you've lost someone you love,
And there's an empty space;
Fill it with your memories,
Put them all in place.

Then every time you enter the room,
A lovely glow will appear;
And then you'll have the one you love,
Always so close and so near.

Just a little thing like a smile,
A touch, a warm embrace;
Can make that feeling all worth while,
And will put it all back into place.

You need never feel all alone,
Because you'll have your friends;
With memories burning in your mind,
You'll feel a lot less pain.

Then what you once thought was gone,
Will be there with you always;
You'll find your life will carry on,
With some joy each and every day.

Remember that one day you will once more,
Hold hands and be together;
You'll sit in peace on those far-off shores,
Where tears will be gone forever.

Thelma Cook

17th June

Little Girls

When I was a little girl, my parents said to me,
'When you grow up, oh little one, what do you think you'll be?'
'I think I'll be an actress and work on the silver screen.'
But now that I've grown up, I know that it was just a dream.
For little girls grow up and find their dreams may not come true,
as there is always something else that they have got to do.
But I don't think those dreams should ever really go away,
you should keep them deep inside and never let them stray.
For little girls they see things so very differently,
and I think as we grow older we somehow cease to see.
But the fundamental things in life are very rarely free,
and you have to work so very hard to be who you want to be.
So if you think your life's gone wrong and you feel a bit like me,
remember little girls can dream and be who they want to be.

Julie L Bushell

The Healing Garden

Enter the sun-washed garden
　　in which you lose yourself
among sweet-scented blossoms
　　in sparkling rainbow hues.

Silvered dewdrops
　　clinging like strings of pearls
on velvet petals
　　soft as angel wings.

Shadowed arbours
　　swathed in sweet seclusion
invite the soul to shed
　　its weary burden.

While merry crystal water sprites
　　dance in exuberant ecstasy
to merge with pools
　　of deep reflection.

Joyous sounds quivering
　　on the gentle breeze
performed by winged musicians
　　bid the soul to stand
in breathless admiration.

And in the woodlands'
　　soft blue velvet
drapes the ground
　　in tender tranquil surrender.

While tall strong guardians
　　veiled in verdant green
unfurled their slender branches
　　in silent benediction.

Enter this enchanted garden
　　in which you find yourself
And heal your wounded heart.

Brigitta D'Arcy

River Of Life

As I stand upon the bridge
and watch the river flowing
I wonder where it comes from
and where is it going?

It reminds me of God's love
ever flowing full and free,
reaching out to all mankind,
flowing out through you and me

One day we'll reach that river
that's beside God's heavenly throne,
where we'll dwell with Him forever
in our eternal home.

Our worries will be over,
there will be no more tears or strife,
as we cross that healing river,
clear as crystal, the river of life.

Margaret Clifford

Child Of God

Child of God
You have sadly bent but
Have not been broken
With the ravages of time
You have bent
As a reed bends
So fragile
With the passing of time
As the sun repairs the reed
To stand firm again
So you, my child
Will stand firm as
The sun begins to shine
Caressing your frame to
Be stronger now and able
To stand the strain and pain
That life sometimes
Throws our way
So child of God
Smile again
You have bent but
Have not been broken
With the ravages of time.

Penny Kirby

20th June

Sunset

I never see the sun go down
But I think of the end of all things made:
The day is dead, the night now reigns
And sleep will bring an end to pains.

For human pains are hard to bear;
Throughout the living day and the lonely eve,
Our conscious soul is wracked by care
But gentle night brings peace from fear.

All things must die, all grows old;
This must be so, no other way.
So make the one life you're given to lead
As good and true as in your head.

Ian Mason-Smith

Loss

(For Emma and Samantha who lost someone close to their hearts)

When people we love pass away
Our lives turn upside down and are never the same
Sleepless nights and cold sweats
Deep sad sorrow, many regrets
Things we put off for another day
Are now long overdue and harder to say
So to people you love never miss a chance
Go to the cinema or sit in the park
Or stay up all night to watch a sunrise with someone you love
And to yourself always be true
And always remember someone out there also loves you.

Daniel Leader

Faith

Swooning with starlight - sparkling and heady champagne -
Dazed with the sweet dark wine of a western sea,
As in dim ages I knew, I know once again
The oneness, the mystic enchantment, of life's unity.

The flimsy grey wisps that flush rose in an amethyst sky,
The flower that slowly expands to the heat of the sun,
Are they not part of a wholeness they cannot deny,
A beauty that knits all its diverse members in one?

Past generations are one with the child yet unborn;
Do not fear, for the stars with the hopes of the world are bright.
The dream in the soul and the dream that created the dawn
Are one, and together make music out of the night.

Joyce Tweedie

Bound Soul And Spirit

When the night has come and gone,
think of Me, Thy Lord and Son.
In all weathers see Me beside you -
in the mist of dawn,
in the rays of the summer sun,
in My raiment.
Know that it is really Me
each new-day morning.
See, I am always to be found
when each day is done -
each evening.
So you see Me all the time,
I am never from you.
Each and every hour
I am there for you.
The sombre spirits of the night
may haunt you,
but I am by your side.
I watch 'til morning comes.
So dance the night away
and see the dawn rise fully again.
Come, follow Me,
take heart for the journey to come.
Just follow Me,
for you know I am with you.
Just follow.

Anne Hadley

Feeling For Eternity

If wondering *can find a meaning in the life we live*
then when you wonder how you feel
then it must be shared
as whatever you feel,
could mean everything to you
so if you hold it tight close to your heart
it will never leave you.

If something means everything to you
you must hold it tight
that you take it,
to everywhere and everyone you know
to someone,
it will mean the world
trust it, believe it
it will make you.

You may think this thought
has abandoned you.
but if you search deep inside
you feel that everything
you wonder will appear,
as a thought that can
make your life an eternal joy.

Amy Herbert (14)

Life's Pathway

Our lives are like the seasons often changing day by day
With all the highs and lows of living as along its path we wend our way
You look out of the window, watch winter-grey clouds go scudding by
Our thoughts just seem to match them so low there in the sky
When suddenly appears a robin with breast so red it glows
You catch your breath in wonder, watch it hopping to and fro
This little scene uplifts you, making your day more bright
You are thankful for your warm house, food, your cosy bed at night
Then wander into springtime, more hope within our hearts
The flowers, trees and hedgerows start blossoming at last
Tiptoe into glorious summer, skies so blue, cotton wool clouds sail by so white
Our lives now so much brighter, our worries manifestly light
Progression next to autumn with jewelled colours, oranges, reds and golds.
We stand in awe of nature, like our lives as its swath unfolds
Hand in hand we travel, God always by our side
We pray to Him, He listens and will always be our guide.

Marjorie Leyshon

Solar Power

As my solar thoughts
in five minutes of darkness
enlighten to blue, red, yellow and white jewels
I think of rock gardens with solar flowers
powered by the sunlight
in bright and subtle colours
but displayed only in pots or hanging towers
as we need to breathe
while plants do so much goodness
to planet Earth and give out oxygen
perhaps dispersed round the patio or garden ponds
with people drinking green tea and ginger
under lighted floral parasols
and eating different-flavoured ice cream
at seaside tables
people in Lycra swimwear
with flowing rainbow chiffon sarongs
gaudy shorts and longs.

Gina A Miller

You Will Not Be Leaving

(Written when my mother's home of over fifty years had to be sold in 2003 and she had no choice but to go into a nursing home)

When I close your door for
the final time and walk away,
the light will go out on that day,
but you will not be leaving.
That would be too cruel, too harsh
and stop me from believing
that your very breath and being, contained
in bricks and mortar in those walls,
as finally the darkness falls,
will wait until one day
to gently tremble by the neck
of an unwary stranger and lay
his unspoken fears to rest as he
brushes aside this butterfly's kiss,
a touch which he will probably dismiss,
yet shivering, will pause, his senses reeling –
could imagination play such tricks,
embrace him with such warmth of feeling?
That same stranger may well in his dreams
catch the sound of distant laughter,
awakening suddenly so shortly after,
glimpse a drop of water trickling from the sky
down a pane of glass – yet there is no rain –
and taste the salty sadness and will cry.
Your courage in sustaining life with
all the odds hard-stacked against you,
(your silent pleas for help were very few),
must never be consigned to dust.
Who else to recognise and tell your story?
I, while I can – the stranger must.

Angela R Davies

A Daughter

What is a daughter?
A delight,
Both to the heart and to the sight,
From infancy to older days,
So feminine in all her ways,
Caring so well for doll and teddy,
Chockfull of interest, always ready
To join us both doing our work,
Quite irksome jobs she doesn't shirk . . .
She grows, and adds to all her skills -
She knits, she swims, she sews, she trills:
She loves to play, she loves to sing,
She'll turn her head to anything.
Alone, with Mum or Dad, a book
She so enjoys, and loves to cook,
Revelling in everything she'll learn,
Acquiring facts at every turn.
. . . Then, all too soon, she's flown the nest
As children do, like all the rest,
To make of life whate'er she will,
Of life's enjoyments takes her fill.
A wider group of friends and neighbours
She meets through leisure and through labours,
And, as her busy life proceeds,
She still remembers all our needs
With love for us and much concern,
Ready to help at every turn.
When hurt she's brave, resilient too,
When all's against her she'll come through.
Friendships she's made in every quarter -
Our sympathetic, caring daughter.

Janet Bowerman

Friends

Sitting quietly at home
Do not think I am alone
Speaking to my sister dear
I am sure that she is here.

People come and go from me
Sometimes drink a cup of tea
Or, if they go quickly through,
I then know that they are new.

Give me both new friends and old
One is silver, other gold
Things will happen whilst I sleep
So, thank God for those who creep.

Robert S Dell

100%

Don't give up believing
In what you wish to do
Study hard and try your best
And that should get you through

You'll only achieve what you want in life
If you give 100%
But if you don't try hard enough
Later you'll repent

Nothing is impossible
It's all within your reach
Why settle for cherry
When, instead, you could have peach?

Anne Elibol

Ancient Miracle Thoughts

A little thought, through time, passed down,
To raise little smiles, and remove any frown.
When life seems bleak, and feels really blue,
Then here are some things, to try and do.

Think of the good times, within your life,
They should far outweigh any trouble or strife,
Look for the happy times, of days gone by,
They will be in there, in memory give it a try.

Remember with thought, those days of laughter,
As they remain to cheer you, forever and after.
It's hard to clear, a heart filled with pain,
And replace it with smiles, to cheer you again.

So bring to mind, the good times, life has brought,
Keep thinking it over, no matter how fraught.
Then sadness and pain will gradually subside,
And be replaced with smiles from memories inside.

It's an ancient age-old ritual, or so I am told,
To cherish any happiness, as precious as gold,
It's a form of special calm, and meditation,
And practised by angels, with sweet dedication.

Good times by far, always outweigh the sad,
Seek these within, for there are many you've had.
If you cannot achieve this, then an idea to lend,
Is to rely and enlist the helpful ear, of a friend.

C R Slater

Crashing Waves

Crashing waves, moving on,
World keeps turning, life soon gone.
The sun rises, the sun sets,
Today, tomorrow, one soon forgets.
A drop of a tear, a broken heart,
Lasts forever? Only to start;
Words of love, cry out in pain,
Yesterday, now you're ashamed.
Can't go back, why bother trying?
Forget it quick, before you're dying.
You're moving on, that's good to see,
No longer lost, that's the way to be.
Stay gone forever, never go back,
Everlasting sun, forbidden black.
Smell of the sea, crash of the ocean,
I feel like my life has finally begun.

Sarah Sproston

Flutterby

(This poem is dedicated to Tara)

How I long for the seasons to change,
To catch a glimpse of you once again.
The autumn leaves pass by my window,
In vibrant colours of orange and gold.
Winter comes and lays a blanket of snow,
Footprints fade from the warmth of the sun.
At last my wait is nearly over,
As the first signs of spring can be seen.
Then suddenly as if by magic you appear,
Silent, so gentle, the summer breeze carries you.
Your fragile wings of velvet taking you higher,
Oh how I envy your freedom of flight.
I watch with wonder as you land,
So close, I wish you could stay.
With quiet thoughts I look from afar,
But all too soon I blink and you're gone.
So every time I see a butterfly,
I think of you and smile.
For although I may not see you every day,
In my heart you will always be with me . . .

B D Nelson

Daily Reflections On Nature

Give thanks for the sun, the wind and the rain,
Give thanks for the crops that feed us again,
The Earth, the roots are fresh with dew,
The grass so green,
Food for the sheep which we have all seen.

Give thanks for the trees which blossom all along,
The birds are chirping, singing their song,
The bees are humming, collecting pollen from the tree,
To make honey for you and me.

Give thanks for the food which gives us strength for body and mind,
Just by giving thanks to God by making us mankind,
Nature looks after itself day by day,
For the farmers who collect for harvest,
And go to church with it today.

Matthew Willbye (16)

Hope

A wondrous object to behold
A golden shining light of hope
A true delight
A precious gift
To be held within a heart.

Some people are black and barren inside
Despair has entered their hearts
A second chance
A helping hand
To feel the warmth of your touch.

Your appearance changes
You begin as a seed
Implanted to grow
Unburden and lift
The spirits of those you touch.

You're a beautiful butterfly
An eternal sphere of golden hope
Bestowing your power
Lighting the dark
Inspiring the souls you touch.

Margo McBirnie

Lazy Days

Thoughts of Crantock, Treslissick Gardens
(shingle beach) and Perranporth - with
Lucy; also a touch of 'Summer Days, Summer Filled Days - 'Grease'.'

Lazy days
Breeze-filled days
Summer sunshine shining steadily down
Sleepy afternoons on sandy, duned beaches
The warmth of the sun relaxing, renewing the senses.

Lazy days
Of quiet country lanes
The patterned sunlight filtering through the trees
Falling down on the retriever's back
The ruts of earth dry under the sandalled feet.

A hum of bees in the honeysuckle
The call of the curlew
A gentle lapping of the water;
Or later, a crashing, a crescendo of waves
As the tide comes quickly in
And the sun disappears behind a menacing cloud.
Rain comes suddenly but has a refreshing touch
Soon the sunshine returns to warm our faces,
Above, wispy white 'angel' clouds fly across the blue sky.

Lazy days
Summer-filled times
Echoes of yesterday
The pleasant present in which we linger
Before tomorrow comes
And the time stretches out to September . . .
Our lazy days become sharpened
By the early morning touch of coolness.
Ah, lazy days, come again, come again.

Anne Veronica Tisley

July

Long, burnished grass,
Copper, feathery tones of sage,
Like a fabric,
Generously on Earth bestowed,

Seen, remembered,
That russet gentle covering,
Until the rain,
Made each stem bow, heads hanging low.

In prime cut down,
Crown of summer in ripeness met,
Yet will renew,
True to the seasons' interchange.

Harvested, bound,
Rounds of gold standing fresh minted,
Waiting for wraps,
Like items from the summer sales.

Kathleen M Scatchard

Broken

You broke me.
I was angry.

I was confused and though
You listened, You stayed quiet
And didn't explain.

I cried every day.
You collected up my tears
But didn't stop them from flowing.

I hated myself.
You carried on loving me
But I never really heard You say so.

I felt guilty.
You forgave me a long time ago
But I couldn't always be sure.

I punished myself
And You let me continue
But protected me from going too far.

I was lost
And You took me through
Such a harsh path to be found again.

But You did explain, comfort and love me.
You did forgive, protect and guide me.
And You waited for the right time.

You set me free and brought me home.
You pushed me as far as You safely could.
You changed my heart, O God.

You broke me.
I am grateful.

Tessa Jane Lee

When I

When I looked forwards you were the one
When I looked forwards you gave me fun
When I looked backwards you were my lover
When I looked backwards you were mine for ever
Now we're apart I need you most
Now we're apart you are just my ghost
When I look forward my life is sad
When I look forward I feel so bad
When I wake up I love you dearly
When I look up I feel you nearly
But life goes on I won't forget you
But life goes on I'm glad I met you
Now I look forward my life seems bright
Now I look forward you are still my life
Now I look backwards you gave me so much
Now I look forwards I'm glad we're in touch
      I will always love you

Lesley Hoddy

A Golden Wedding Anniversary
Where Went The Time?

(Written for my 50th wedding anniversary, 5th July 2004)

What of my youth, which departed in a flash,
I was only a blushing lad, trying to cut a dash.
Oh, that magic moment of a flirtatious first kiss,
And the warm, soft embrace of young lovers' bliss.

This led to wedding vows, while church bells chimed,
Struggling to establish a home with all efforts combined.
Perpetual daily labours, turning the weeks into years,
With successes, failures, happiness - and the tears.

Blessed with sweet children which came our way,
But not the nights awake when they wanted to play.
Recalling the happy hours with their laughter ringing,
Through all the seasons, when life seemed to be singing.

Remember the hard times when money wasn't there,
The many nights awake worrying in utter despair.
There were even sadder times, when moved to weeping,
When friends and loved ones passed into God's keeping.

Forgive the fights and the words spoken with regret,
Times of anger when wedding vows weren't met.
There are rewards, in forgiveness and understanding,
Learning to be more tolerant, kind, and less demanding.

Recall all the good times with companionship sharing,
Of compassion and kindness, and their generous caring.
The years create a trust and the union strengthens still,
Fifty years seem to have gone quickly since I said, 'I will.'

John Mitchell

A Cry In The Night

Night's silver queen sails cold, serene, across a sea of space.
My baby's countenance is seen mid pillows edged with lace.
O tranquil peace, please last till dawn; my child through slumber safely borne.
Still undisturbed she, unperturbed, displays a peaceful face.

Then silence flees with rising breeze as clouds block out the light:
My baby frowns as tossing trees are rocked to left and right.
A distant flash, a thunder boom, another crash lights up the room:
With further quakes the child awakes and cries out in the night.

As danger nears I kiss those tears, soft in my arms she'll lay.
To drown the storm and calm her fears, I sing and softly pray,
The child is fed and nursed and changed, her crumpled cot is rearranged;
With tender care and whispered prayer, her sulks are soothed away.

Birdsong I hear as dawn draws near: away my foolish qualm!
The rain has gone, but still my tune sounds in the morning calm.
A peaceful change comes with the sun, and order is from chaos won.
Through storm and sway, God lights the way and brings us safe from harm.

F Jeffery

Target

The morn's gone by wi muckle laughter
gone beside the lave wa past;
'tis minutes syne we left the ithers –
thocts an laughter dinna last!
Ma hert's resoondin wi the laughter –
the warld's sae comely when it's there.
A feel a want anither session
but fine a ken there'll be nae mair.
Ye canna spend yeir life in laughin
the grim necessity's aye there
tae keep yeir een aye on the target
or else ye'll find life cauld an bare!
The target varies man tae man –
tae preserve yeir ain, enjoy the moment;
help the next ane if ye can!
We'll meet again, if God's so willin
and laughter will again be bright
though dark the road ti whaur we're gaun
the end will be celestial light!

Andrew Duncan

Symbols Of Love

Flickering candles on the altar stand
Symbols of love in a faraway land
Young men are fighting, for things they believe
Will bring peace, harmony, no more to grieve.
Flickering candles on the altar stand
We question this war in a faraway land
To pray for these young men, the dangers they face
We ask God to guide them, and keep them safe.
Flickering candles on the altar stand
Will there ever be peace in this faraway land?
And the candles that flicker, so brightly each one
Are symbols of love for a husband or son.
Flickering candles on the altar stand
Mothers and daughters in this faraway land
How will they bring peace? Can they stop this war
And make the land safe, as it was before?

Gillian Doble

No Gold Or Silver

I possess the greatest of treasures
Sadly some people never have a true friendship
Have no one to tell them about their pressures
Or no one by them when sorrow has her grip
Someone to share laughter with
But also there through all the tears
Turn to you when I can't kin and kith
And I need to allay my fears
When you need comfort I'm there
I can't think of anything better than to help a friend
And let them know you care
Also in their time it's great to spend
    If my ship never comes in
    With you as a friend I already win.

Jeff Brooks

Turning Back

Crossing the bridge won't be easy,
But one thing at least you'll have learned,
As long as it's there for the crossing,
It means that the bridge you've not burned.
It's so easy when pushing life forwards,
And living one side of the track,
To wipe all the footsteps behind you,
Thinking you'll never look back.
Catching a glimpse of tomorrow,
In yesterday's mirror today,
Loving the one in a million,
Losing's the price you won't pay.
If everyone lived for the moment,
Then the moment, when it has gone,
Would leave us the dark side of nowhere,
In a world where the light seldom shone.
To be honest, it's plain and it's simple,
Whatever you did yesterday,
Will be written in stone by tomorrow,
You can't wipe that slate clean, no way.

J Brohee

Understanding

Sometimes you stare blankly,
not seeing at all.
Confused and so frightened,
then the mask starts to fall.

So much emotion,
yet you feel no pain.
So much to give,
so little to gain.

When you feel love,
you push it away.
The anger's too strong,
to keep it at bay.

The frustration you feel,
I also feel too.
Why can't you love me
the way I love you?

When I try to hold you,
you just turn away.
Oh please do not hurt me,
if only for one day.

And although it's a struggle
that has just begun.
I will never give up,
because you are my son.

Maria Brough

The Woods Are Full Of It

trumpets are sounding

tarara in the forest you ween
turtles are flying above your tent
of hammering forelocks in the wind
no it's trees, trees pure and simple
mind you they make imbrications
in the thickets

there they go wild rabbits
hiding in the scrub brush
that is they are called somehow
to screen you from their beaded eyes
hop, they vanish

the red-tailed hawk is flying
floating on a drought of air
see them there
him and his mate
they're searching out rodents
for breakfast

All of the clamour is still
as of this moment you hear the leaves
there's mystery in that

Christopher Mulrooney

Paradox Of Powerlessness

'Come down, from the cross,
come on, come down,
You saved all the others,
yet You can't save Yourself.'

Let's have fun, in the sun.
Men die, men cry,
men scream, 'Why me?'
Taunts, torture, mocking, glee.

A hand to be nailed, pierced,
cast stars into space,
A voice crying with passion, 'Father forgive,'
created the beauty in the world where we live.

Yes, You could have come down,
from the strong cross of shame,
crushed us with the spectacular
and not borne our pain.

But You gave us freewill
to love You and adore,
to accept or reject,
what could You have done more?

Dorothy Brooks

Résumé

I don't know how long has gone by
since your offer of sunshine
transformed me and this life of mine.
You have written your signs
wherever I turn my eyes,
the vertical trees in the changes of light,
the garden yielding to the rhythm of season,
the flight of birds in the variable sky.
You have written your signs within me.
There is nothing within and without
which is mine.
Your eternal yes
is signing all time and space
and it will forever sunshine
on your resurrection.

Angela Matheson

Country Roads

Five-bar gates and tall green hedges
Fields of crops swaying in the breeze
Roadside ditches lined with sedges
Tall slim poplars dance and tease.

Crooked white signposts mark the way
Along narrow winding roads and lanes
To all the little villages and hamlets
Left wet and muddy by the rains.

Thatched roof cottages nestle here
Trimmed with roses, honeysuckle and mint
Where the village pub has a duck pond
And a trough for farm horses to drink.

Time seems to stand still in these places
And beauty by God's been bestowed
Fleetingly, you too can be part of it
Just take time to travel down -
- Country roads.

John Osland

Time To Say

When 'they' say, 'You can't do this
You're getting old,'
Then's the time to say . . .
'The years, my friend, are sliding by
But look at what I've got;
A wealth of happy memories,
Skills you've not yet learnt,
The knowledge now to say
This time I'll not get burnt.'

When 'they' say, 'You can't eat that
You'll get fat,'
That's the time to say . . .
'Fat's a word I do not know
'Ample', maybe - yes, today,
But I'm happy with who I am.
I've done my bit of being thin
And the time has come to show,
Life does not begin and end with being slim!'

When 'they' say, 'You can't climb a mountain
You'll break your neck,'
Now's the time to say,
'The birds have grown and flown the nest
I have the will, I have the knowledge,
I have the time, the world is mine.
I'll learn to swim, I'll learn to fly
The world's my oyster
To explore, before it's time to die.'

Yvonne Bulman-Peters

Sojourn In Oblivion

Life in a world
Where it's more surreal
Than imagination can reach
We can't behave
'Cause no one can teach
We can't react
'Cause nothing is what it seems
Accept everything
Reject nothing
Open minds can only receive
Who is to know?
If it's not meant to deceive
Observe it, be it,
And only then can you know it
We are all on a journey
To the unknown
Until we get there
It won't be home
A sojourn in oblivion it can be
Only when you wake up
You have to face reality!
And spend the day
Wishing for that eternity
Dreaming where you can never go
In your mind you know
That sleepy world in your head
Has gone to oblivion.

David McDonald

Grass Is Never Greener

The grass is never greener on the other side of town.
Man's non-existent fantasy - the same old shade of brown.

Often what you really need lies right beneath your eyes,
Obscured by past experience - by other people's lies.

Reality is not green grass made bright by summer sun,
But gentler like a flowing stream, whose depths have distance run.

Leave be the brilliant fairy lights - they are just what they seem,
Fragile shells of sharded glass where someone else has been.

Pick up the sward beneath your hand, look at it again,
Seeing it barely as it is, may ease away the pain.

It may not seem so glittering the gift you found today,
But take it, as you find it, before - it slips away.

Leigh Crighton

A Summer's Day

The sun edges across the purest of skies,
With neither a ripple nor a wink of imperfection.
It moves silently on its bed of deep, deepest blue,
Swimming, gliding, across the sky for all below.
And the obedient shadows follow suit,
Edging across the purest of things,
Creating jealousy and relief in their wake.
And the flowers reach out to touch their sun,
With hands of lilac and ruby and deepest purple,
Against the purest blue.
The soft purr of the winged choir enlightens the guilty crevice,
As the sun continues its most innocent journey,
On this pure and most beautiful day.

Matthew Richards

A Midsummer's Relax

Such a peaceful feeling,
You get sitting by the sea.
Where the waves lap and ripple,
Singing their deep melody.
Gone are my stresses
Concerns and all that depresses
My mind just free
Ready to be filled with my poetry!
I lean my head back
Letting the sunshine upon my face
Opening my eyes gradually
To see the real beauty of this place.
Rugged landscape, white-capped cliffs
Where the ocean meets the land.
England sees so much of creation at its best
Her pebble banks and golden sand.
Seagulls fly ahead
You can hear their laugh and call.
I hope you can take the time
This summer, to sit and enjoy it all!

Michelle Luetchford

Peace Of Mind

The world is not perfect, why should it be?
But somehow, it seems to suit you and me.
There is earth and water and light and air,
But they have to be used with sense and flair.

If your life is focused on things to buy,
You have no hope of finding peace.
There is always a bigger and smarter car,
That is just that bit out of your reach.

There is no point in envying those,
Who grasp everything from above,
The rest of us find our joy on this Earth
In feelings, and friendship, and love.

It is hard to resist a quote from the past,
But Omar said years ago,
That happiness is simply a glass of wine,
Under a bough, with one that you know.

Is it just chance, or is there a God,
Who arranges things, without fuss?
The answer is lost in the mists of time
And may never be revealed to us.

John Troughton

The 'Inner' Core

The apple can have a red or green peel,
Both of which have a certain appeal
Its 'inner' is the important part,
The main centre – the very heart.

Much the same can be said of humans too,
Our hearts, our souls – not often on view;
But if we look deep, what do we see?
Us, our lives.
Does this make us stand still, or do we run free?

Free as a bird to fly away,
Experiencing our life through work and play.

Time goes by
Until we realise
That returning home – is where we need to be,
In order to make our lives totally complete.

Cheryl Campbell

Listen To Your Heart

You know the kind of problems
that we get from day to day,
what to do or where to turn
or 'just what should I say?'
The trouble is, there's no right way
to tackle each new task
and sometimes you will hesitate
or be afraid to ask
but each and every one of us
has, deep down inside
a gift that has the answer
or gives us all a guide.
All we have to do is listen
and the outlook gets much brighter.
The problem that was there before
now suddenly seems much lighter.
So remember, when you need some help
the easiest way to start
is simply take a little time
and listen to your heart.

Donald Ferguson

The Light Doth Lighten My Darkness

(. . . the Lord will lighten my darkness . . .' 2 Samuel 22-29 AV)

The Lord doth lighten my darkness
My loneliness, despair
When everyone's against me
And no one seems to care.

The Lord doth lighten my darkness
'Neath deep financial strain
I turn to Him for wisdom
To meet each pressing claim.

The Lord doth lighten my darkness
When sickness takes its hold
I lean upon His bosom
And there my hurts unfold.

The Lord doth lighten my darkness
When I'm misunderstood
I turn to Him for comfort
For I His love have proved.

The Lord will lighten my darkness
Whatever life may bring
To Him. 'Eternal refuge'
My fragile heart doth cling.

Jennifer René Daniel

I'm Standing Here

I'm standing here beside you, now.
I hear your earnest plea.

Be still and know that I am God,
Who created all and thee.

I will not let you go before
a trial you cannot stand.

Be sure to know that I will guide,
and help you understand.

That this must come and this must go.
This just had to pass,

for all things work together, child,
if your love for me lasts.

Stray not to either side, dear one,
neither left nor to the right.

The battle for your soul is on,
and I'll take on the fight.

Trust in me a thousand times
and then seventy times more.

Walk the path as I would walk,
'til last you reach my door.

Think not that I've forsaken thee,
in your darkest hour.

I'm merely waiting for the joy,
to transfer you My power.

'Lean not unto your own understanding . . .
and I shall direct thy paths!' (Prov. 3.6)

Mike Herman

Now

Live for the present
Enjoy every day
Settle for the here and now
Do not delay
Dream about the future
If you really must
But now is the real gift
It's the only thing to trust
So store it in your memory
Don't forget
It's only now that's important
So do not fret.

Katherine Parker

Cheryl's Poem

She's potty about her garden,
She potters there all day long,
Planting things and cutting things
Till the sun has been long gone.
She wakes up in the morning,
Looks outside her window frame,
If the sky is leaden and the rain is falling
She feels like she's gone lame.
But look at her when the sun is shining
And she's pottering in her garden,
She's got no time for anything else
And for this she makes no pardon.
So leave her there to potter
In her garden full of bliss,
Where the plants all vie for attention
And the feel of the sun's sweet kiss.
For this is God's sweet Eden
And she knows if she tends it with love,
He'll be pottering getting things ready,
In His garden up above.

Christine Storey

A Different Stair

Of many stairs, I've climbed, to see
How very different life can be.
When very young on crawling fours
To adventures fast on romantic shores.
Then as mystery grows those creaking ones
'Who is it? Who goes there?' no one knows
Then of lofty climbs, in houses bold
Where - great men hid from many foes
Stairs fashioned - of regent style
When ladies woed, climbed up to rile
But those were the ones, when swordsmen parried
Sliding down banisters, never to be married
Of empty silent - fairer mansions
As doors creaked open, dust lay in sanctions
To tread its flights, a miracle to survive,
It shuddered and swayed, memories alive
Of yesteryear when all was swank
The music echoed, the stairs just shrank
Of overweight waistcoats and powdered hair
And dancers strove to music rare
Of elegant, graceful stairs that cause
The heart to race at its beautiful flair
What circular, winding, binding angles
As to Heaven it seems to meander
Of mystic murders, stairs of Hell
Thrown from heights, never to tell
How wonderful - stairways - such a flight that reach
From Earth to Heaven, aglow with His light
Treading the rise, searching and reaching
Each one revealing, His word and teaching.

Albert Boddison

When All Is Still

Sometimes when all is still
In the darkness of the night
I often feel you close to me
And saying I'm alright.

Sometimes when all is still
When the sun decides to shine
The shadows in the garden form
And your face looks down on mine.

Sometimes when all is still
And I try to get to sleep
You hold me gently in your arms
And I can feel at peace.

Sometimes when all is still
And I feel that I can't cope
I feel your hand take hold of mine
And whisper I'm alright.

Sylvia Goodman

'Excuse Me, Have We Met Before?'

You pull me towards you,
Loss and desperation pass, reunited at last.
We've walked this earth for centuries,
Sometimes whole, sometimes not.
'Yes my love, we've met many times before.'

Parts of the same soul sent back to do a job,
To make the world a better place for all of us to have.
Some people call us angels, some say we're born again,
Recycled, says my little girl, certain
She's been here many times before.

To value and love life is all that I can tell,
Each species just as precious and not ours to kill.
Until Earth is as Heaven our promise undone.
The spirits of an angel will return many times again,
Till there's peace on this planet between animals and men.

Barbara Balmer

Communing

I gaze at the sky and seek to commune
With the stars and the birds, the sun and the moon,
I look up to Heaven where my destiny lies,
To know Nature's secrets, to be kind and wise.

I probe human minds and try to read hearts,
For in human kindness is where loving starts,
In ancient men's visions, in folklore and dreams,
In crystal cool waters and quick-flowing streams.

In innocent songs and the eyes of a child
Mother Earth is respected and forests grow wild,
In simplicity - living and bread that is shared,
In joyful young mothers whose breasts can be bared.

The milk of divinity flows free from such breasts,
And a babe in full trust there suckles and rests,
A hope for mankind, life calling its own,
A place of true peace, love nurtured and known.

We men must become indeed need to be,
The 'Mothers', the 'Guardians' of Man's destiny,
New births now await us, the world must be fed,
And those of the flock to safety be led.

The world is a-changing, it's mobile and strange,
Our scope must now widen, embrace vaster range,
We must help this Season, become the midwives
Of peaceful new blossoms, protected young lives.

Emmanuel Petrakis

The Journey

How far is it to Bethlehem?
Well, now I'm rather old,
I've had the chance to go there,
And I'm not completely sold.
Not much peace and beauty there,
Goodwill to all on Earth,
But troops, and anger, strife, and stress
To mark the Saviour's birth.
And yet, and yet, the Saviour came
Not to a place at ease,
But one just like the one I saw,
Soldiers, barricades, and thieves.
How far is it to Bethlehem?
As far as you can make it,
A million miles, a few short steps,
For those who truly take it.
For Christ, the Lord, came down to Earth,
It doesn't matter where,
Bethlehem or Timbuktu,
Glasgow - Trafalgar Square.
He comes just where you want Him,
He meets you where you are,
No need of lengthy journey,
No need of guiding star.
Just welcome Him beside you,
Believe His promise true,
And that special place you'll find Him
Will be Bethlehem for you!

Jack Scrafton

Dreams

I know that dreams can be fulfilled
Wishes come true that you have willed
You have to chase your heart's desires
Walk, head held high through nightmare fires
Push yourself right to your limit
Grab each chance, hold on tight to it
Keep on driving, going until you've had enough
Yes you can do it! You have to be tough
In yourself you must trust and depend
Then you'll find your pot of gold at the rainbow's end.

Angela C Oldroyd

From Your Humble Servant

Forgive me Lord for any doubts, that I have shown today,
And thank you for your kindness, in showing me the way,
To help the people that I meet, to teach them of your love,
Guiding them through prayer and song, sent to you above,
Give me the strength to carry on, to follow where you lead,
Lord I ask your blessings to help the ones in need,
Patience and understanding, for those with troubled minds,
No selfish thoughts to taint the day, to always remain kind,
I ask all this of you my Lord, for I am human too,
And strive to carry out your work, the best that I can do.

Kathleen Townsley

Inner Wonder

Why is it some people just cannot decide
The type of person that they are deep inside?
And is this the reason for their demise?
It depends on the problem and how to deal with its size

Some go through their day with feelings of wonder
Why we get depressed? Someone puts us under
We should look at the reasons, maybe we will see
Our minds have a choice and that's how it should be

Just thinking positive, you'll find you can master
Any job that you get or doom or disaster
Deal with each day as if it were your last
Then the fear of the heart will soon be surpassed

Smile and think now is this really me?
No matter whatever I'm going to be free
Try laughing and joking be happy throughout
You know negative thoughts you're better without

Now you've realised your very own wonder
So live out your life like the rain to thunder
Show the whole world it's better to be
The wisest of men for the whole world to see.

Stephen C Matthews

C'est La Vie!

Time to get up for work again,
Don't really want to go,
Keep up the pace, put on a brave face,
Don't let my feelings show.

Time to smile, but all the while,
Don't want to smile at all,
Jump out of bed, lipstick red,
Really feel quite small.

One step forward, two steps back,
All those letters to send,
Stress may cause a heart attack,
When will the nightmare end?

Reflect a moment, but it's gone,
Just like yesterday,
Modern watch, it's a Swatch,
Time just slips away.

What is the meaning of our lives?
Humdrum, yes that rhymes,
So does birth and Christmas mirth,
And happy wedding day chimes.

Spread a little happiness,
Try and forget the past
Have some fun, here comes the sun
It's holiday time at last.

Josie Pepper

In His Glorious Presence

There is a home in Heaven
To all who pass that way,
Where angels are heard singing
As on their harps they play,
A standing ovation is given
The saints bid all to come,
Enter the glorious presence
Of God and His wonderful Son.

A place that knows no sickness
Neither is there pain,
No more do they feel heartache
Just joy in abundance to gain,
Sorrow from earthly frustrations
Are not known in Heaven above,
Nor sadness that brings tears
Only peace in the kingdom of love.

No saint will ever grow weary
Old age shall never be known,
For all are blessed with eternal youth
Up there in their heavenly home.
May the God of peace bring rest
As you look to where your loved one has gone
For they have entered the glorious presence
Of God and His wonderful Son.

Paula E Kewin

Compelling Journey

Sound and colour are synonymous in that they represent same aspects of the same spectrum. Vibrations give us the simplicity of understanding, and the realisation and quality from within our understanding and perception of life forms, that all lives and breathes is subjected to birth and death. Continuity and diversity constitutes and enables the species to form and manifest in totality in the essence of the cosmos. The evolutionary path begins by entering through many aspects into matter, to perform its true ideal creativity, all the information as required to fulfil its obligation for that particular period in time. Regardless of divisions which alternate at inconsistent levels when the times comes which is inevitable all pass the way of affliction and decomposition into realms of obscurity? Physical life becomes extinct and passes through that transformation which for a better word we call Death. But that which dwells within the realm of its inner depths is released and awakened into perfection, taking with it all the experiences in that particular life, to become one with the cosmos, on the long journey through time and space. There is no end only continuity through trial and error. No dogma as yet comes to terms with this phenomena from one who has ventured with reasonable clarity upon His path.

Matthew Wilson

Life Is A Struggle

Many of us, including me,
Suffer from, muscular dystrophy,
Each single day, we feel great pain
But very rarely, do we complain.

Those of you, who don't understand,
Try to give, a helping hand,
We appreciate it, so very much,
It really is, a caring touch.

Most of the time, we seem to smile,
But sometimes blue, once in a while,
We really, cannot tell you why,
But sometimes, we need to sit and cry.

Only the same, can understand,
But yes, we need a helping hand,
We are, too proud to ask for help,
Sometimes we fall, and give a yelp.

So if we seem, to be offhand,
It's only like walking, in quick sand,
So if we seem, to be a quitter,
Please don't think, we're being bitter.

We really do, appreciate life,
And hold onto it, with all our might,
Sometimes we might, not be too sure,
But live in hope, some day there's a cure.

Kay Dawn Tonks

Humiliation

(Dedicated to Allan)

You speak of humiliation
And how hard it is to bear
But from humiliation
Comes humility

Humility: not humbleness

Humility is grace -
A gift
A reasoning of mind
Of soul

Humility will show ourselves
From a very different view
And give us strength of
Will and purpose

Humility is grace
A treasure
A test of body
And of soul

Humility: not humiliation

Sue Percival

I Told You So

I know it hurts right now, but I am here to listen
Though your heart is in pain my arms are here to hold you
Though you feel ashamed I will stand by you no matter what
For I love you no matter what

When the stones start flying I'll shelter you
When the words start hurting I'll block their sounds with laughter
When they point the fingers of accusation I'll turn you around
For I am here to make the hurts disappear

It won't last long, though it may feel it will
The hurt will, but soon the dark clouds will be gone
And once more you will fly in the sunshine
And feel the sun upon your back

And I will be there also
To see you shine again like a bright star
And they will be unable to look at you as you shine so brightly
And I will smile and say, 'I told you so.'

Ann-Marie Spittle

Oasis

It's time to arise
just to melt hibernation
and breathe deep with relief
but this time inside the lungs.
The clock has announced mutation
for releasing all scales
for walking in loud, fearless voices
to proclaim new salvation.
The moment is set for truth,
I'm back; the spell is broken.
Ice and flames are all gone and tears are dry and forgotten
I finally left the sand;
The ugly duckling became swan
and was called to useful pond
I am unburied; I belong
I am really now alive!

Mario J Torres

Daily Reflections

Silence

Blood and bones and flesh and minds
all in one cacophony of rhythmic perfection

symphony!

Then pause, then peace, then finally release.
Silence is not death but life remembered.

Life remembered.

Raj Mohindra

They Say Don't Be Blue

But think blue –

Hyacinth perfume,
Bluebells' cool haze in a copse
Harebell wafted on a stem so fine
that will not snap
Soon followed by cornflowers' strength.

Summer sea breezes, skies
And eyes.

Baby clothes, candles, a birthday card
Jumper warm and
The cover of a book not yet read.

Ruth Mary Hobson

Where The Echoes Kiss

(Dedicated to my grandfather, Jack Bromwell)

Show me the forest,
Where the echoes kiss,
Where the evergreens
Answer our call.

Where the colours of time,
Turn eternal but never fade
And the patterns of nature
Are repainted with each birth.

Where death is no destruction,
Only the movement between forms,
As life's energy flows through us
But cannot end at our end.

Show me the forest,
Where echoes kiss.
Where leaves tumble on the breeze
And in falling, ask to begin again.

Lindsey Bromwell

The Mantle

Not well tonight,
perplexed and over-tired,
feeling stressed.
Approach your life-long friend
and he will place
a green mantle of healing
around your shoulders.
A cape softly sheened
as the waters of Lake Galilee,
greened and silvered
in the setting sun's hues.
Meet with him there,
just before you fall asleep . . .

that's what I do
and soon I feel better, safer
as faith takes me to his side.

Saviour of the world
and Heaven's crowned King,
he's still the same young man
who walked by his beloved lake,
changeless and unchanging still.
And he will meet you there,
so with faith's mantle
around your shoulders,
you will sleep in tranquillity,
gathering fresh confidence
and serenity.

M Munro Gibson

The Blessings Of Faith

10th August

The only thing in life that is constant is change,
so embrace the changes this year may bring,
for nothing stays the same forever.

Look to the future with hope of better things to come,
don't dwell in the past for what is done is done.

And the seasons of life will change with the
passing of the years;
look to the future with hope and faith,
never stopping to count your fears.

Hold onto the faith that you cherish,
with all the comfort it will bring.
For God's blessings are a precious gift
that makes the soul to sing.

Sing your alleluias and praise the Lord,
for the blessings that He brings.
And when the trials of life come to pass,
you will be rising in God's love,
content to find His peace,
flying without wings like a captive finding release.

Robert Waggitt

Summer Months

Here come the summer months
Brighter mornings, longer nights
Clear blue skies and fluffy clouds
Children paddling in water pools
Trying to keep nice and cool
Adults lounging in the grass
Watching as the time goes past
Lover strolling hand in hand
Walking across the golden sands.

Lorraine Booth

The August Breeze!

She kissed me and captured my breath,
Perhaps I was stood in her way!
Encompassing me in an instant,
She blew twisted sadness away.
Arms open wide I embraced her,
Feeling her touch all of me.
Her touch wasn't mine for the keeping,
But needless to say 'I felt free'.
And the sunshine that followed,
As she bid clouds 'Goodbye!'
Seemed the brightest I'd seen,
From a gorgeous blue sky!
Crisp and fresh like her kiss,
Was the way the world felt!
When the August breeze kissed,
And made my heart melt.

Sid 'de' Knees

Treasured Moments

Cherish the moment when you wake up at dawn
To the song of the birds
As they circle the lawn.

Cherish the smile you receive from a child
The voice of a loved one,
The wind when it's wild.

Cherish the fragrance of the grass and the flowers,
The trees gently swaying,
Enjoy happy hours.

Cherish the sunshine, the air that you breathe,
The snowflakes, the raindrops,
The wind in the trees.

Cherish each breath, each step that you take.
Be grateful for these
As you stroll by the lake.

Cherish your life - you are given but one.
The years pass by so quickly,
So make sure you waste none.

Muriel Roe

Early Morning

Another hot day is dawning
And I must be off down the lane
Where the fiery sun is rising
With the grey-mantled moon still in view
Wildflowers come tumbling down
Still covered with dew
And the grasses show vividly green
As the sun turns a white-golden hue
The sound of a distant train
And the cockerel crows
The people who slumber and sleep
If only they knew
What magic there is down this lane
When the fiery red sun
First comes into view.

Moira Osborn

The Spirit Makes Intercession For Us

Too many words are not correct,
I take each one to use in turn,
And it doesn't ring true,
Some deceit creeps in –
Some inappropriate thing,
And the word goes sadly wrong,
So I call it back and throw it away.
If I say 'this' it might mean 'that'
Or might hurt,
Or might not show
How genuine I am
And silence does not always
Fill the void.
Sometimes the spirit has
To intercede with utterances
Only God can hear.

D M Penhaligon

Home To Heaven

A Mother,
whose raiment was as bright as the sun,
which painted the clouds,
with the same light.
These same clouds,
carried her to Heaven -
her Eternal home,
to be with her Son,
Jesus.
There He crowned,
in His Father's Court,
the one, who bore Him,
Mary, Co-Redemptrix,
Heaven's love -
thanked and praised her.
Alleluia. Alleluia.

E B M Wreede

Angels On High

Angels on high, take the tears that we cry,
Wipe our eyes and let love take command.
Take the hearts that we break, from our endless mistakes,
Show us mercy so we understand.
That dreams we all share, we can grasp if we dare,
Have the courage to stand on our own.
No need to give pain, as we strive hard to gain,
Praise from people, yet none we have known.
Look within you, for the person so true,
Don't be fooled by the masks worn by some.
In a world that disguises all hates, and despises,
The person we all can become!

J M Thomas

Childhood Memories

As I lay in the garden of childhood,
On my back, with my gaze on the sky.
The scent of the flowers around me
And the birds in full song flying by.
I thought it could never have ended
That no one could need ever grow old.
Those winters of warmth and affection
Those long magic summers of gold.
The cedar tree watching above me
Had witnessed my smile and tears
It seemed to have stood there forever
Much longer than human years.
Tho' now when I look at the garden
The flowers have withered away
The cedar is still looking upwards
The songs of the birds are still gay.
The long years have taken my childhood
The loved ones I knew are all dead.
Yet the memories that linger are sweet ones,
The pictures remain in my head.

Brenda P Smith

I Believe

I believe in God
I find it implausible
Not to believe
In His existence.
The Earth and planets
Had to be created
By an intelligent being.
To comprehend eternity
Is difficult and mind-blowing.
My God, what is your nature?
I am still seeking not finding
The answers to my questions.
I hope to discover one day
The truth that eludes me now.
Today it is enough to know that
I believe.

Rose-Mary Gower

I've Been Thinking

Half-asleep and warm and quiet
    My modern thoughts have taken flight –
Back to where my childhood days
    Patterned me in all its ways.

Poor but safe in family care
    Help at hand for all to share;
Kindness shown to all in need,
    Togetherness in word and deed.

Freedom in the country lanes –
    Hopscotch, skipping, growing pains;
Discipline and schooling too,
    Such a lot of things to do.

Sunday - Chapel - voices singing
    'Jesus loves me' still is ringing.
Lessons learned and good deeds done,
    Friendships made and victories won.

Thinking of those days of yore,
    Remembering how it was before,
I know I've learned so many things
    Blessings that true faith still brings.

Bessie Martin

Beauty Under The Skies

Whatever the season beauty survives
Be it spring, autumn, winter or summer skies
Springtime inspires to all creatures new life
Summer florals, berries and fruit that are ripe
Autumn reds and golds decorate bushes and trees
Winters with frosts, snows and rivers that freeze
Fields of green or golden with corn
Fields white with frost or snow on a winter's morn
Trees covered with snow or bursting with bud
Deer with fawn or fox with cub
Birds with fledglings learning to fly
Winged life climbing and diving beneath the sky
Plants, bushes, trees, wildlife, God's creatures all
Beauty under the skies to befall.

Gertrude Schően

Take Your time

You may find it best if you walk with your pride
Than to run from the dreams that you keep deep inside
With the beauty of life that is cheering you on
As it's cheered all the others who have been here and gone
And your mind is now free as you plan your own pace
Cos with no line to cross then it can't be a race.

Shaun Agate

A Smile

A smile on your face will light up the day
For those who receive it on the way
It costs nothing to give but its value is great
Especially to those in a miserable state
It brightens the day bringing a smile in return
Lifts up the spirit of those who are stern
It lightens the load of those full of stress
Just give them a smile to ease their distress
A smile is infectious so spread it around
It is soon returned I have found
So keep on smiling however dull the day
It doesn't cost anything
To blow the blues away

Molly Ann Kean

Be Encouraged

Do not think your cross to put aside
In faithfulness and love you still reside
There is work that you were given still unfinished
And you still have the gifts He gave, the spirit undiminished
So turn again and don't look back
Keep hands firm on the plough
And laugh, and sing and worship Him
For He will show you how

Barbara Harrison

Between The Planets

Between the planets we created a string of hearts,
Never-ending, complete trust,
We packed it tight with all the

Strength of our devotion,
Launched it into Heaven to put the last link in the chain.

Vicky Stevens

Prayer

As this day closes let our thoughts turn to others,
Our close ones, earthly and spiritual sisters and brothers,
Least not forget those who are in our hearts dear,
Shining lights of love, bright, always clear.

Within our prayers each one we call.
None to forget, remembering all,
Thoughts of healing love we project,
Outwards to everyone to protect.

Our prayers, be they simple but with meaning,
Give thanks for our creation and our being.
Prayers of love and of thanksgiving,
For those passed as well for the living.

As sun sets, day turns to dusk,
See light in the darkness, a light we trust.
Feel love in our hearts, pure and strong,
Give it freely, send it where it belongs.

Alan J Morgan

Our Mountains

If I could climb a mountain,
I wonder which it would be,
The Deri or the Sugarloaf,
I'll have to wait and see.

I'd wander up the pathway,
Through fern so tall and green,
I'd look at gentle bluebells,
And breathe the air so clean.

I'd stand upon the mountain top
And look around with pride,
At the Deri and the Sugarloaf
Standing side by side.

There's the Skirrid and the Rholben,
And the Blorange tall and proud,
One day I'm going to climb them all,
And stand upon the peaks,
And then I'll see the beauty
That others come to seek.

Rosemary Caine

His Loving Touch

26th August

God's loving touch comes to our lives
in many different ways
a gentle smile
a loving touch
a word that someone says
a helping hand
an offered prayer
the sun's soft summer rays
these things all gently show His love
to help us through our days.

Daphne E Cornell

Guardian Angel

Guardian angel watching over me
Guide me through life trouble free
Help me distinguish between wrong and right
And keep God's love ever in sight.

Give me strength when strength I need
To fight and win any evil deed
To beat temptation however strong
To do what's right and never to wrong.

Guide me through life like a light so bright
Casting evil to the darkness of night
Keep me safe until my end does come
Then my guardian angel your work is done.

Tony Turner

Your Eyes In The Stars

27th August

See your eyes in the stars
Feel your breath on the breeze
Sense your touch in the rain
Making my heart feel at ease

Catch your tears as they fall
Hear your voice when you call
Know you're here by my side
Please don't run away and hide

Cherished moments to hold
Treasure as precious as gold
As the sun fades on the day
Dream the night away

All our days on this earth
Memories' wealth for all they're worth
One thing we will never lose
Are the hearts of the one that we choose

Glorianna Gee

There's Tomorrow

When life is full of bustle,
With lots of work to do,
    No time to stop
    No time to think
No time to rest, 'tis true.

Remember there's tomorrow,
With hours twenty-four
    To do your work,
    To take a rest,
Of this, you can be sure.

Oh yes, there is tomorrow,
That is another day,
    So take some time
    To stop awhile
Along life's busy way.

And in your time of resting
Come to your Lord in prayer
    He loves you so
    He cares for you
Be sure, He's always there.

Anne Gray

Frozen Ice Cream

They came in cardboard containers, and were different from the others,
Which were pretty-packed in plastic and labelled in litres.
I wondered what they were doing in a nineties supermarket.

I delved into the deep-freeze,
Up to my elbows in full-cream living,
And picked up a pack from its corner of time.

The box had a picture of Dad, Mum and the kids
Laughing, running over sand, as nice and as naff as a bucket and spade,
And the sure blue sky was forty years past its sell-by date.

'Come to Blackpool!' 'Visit Skegness!' 'Make a trip to Burnham-on-Sea!'
These faces were seen on holiday posters on railway stations that smelled of soot,
When Ibiza was foreign and far away and quietly living off fish.

So how could a minnow be still in the swim
While big brands, as big as whales, got better and better
And swallowed up share of moving markets?
This old firm, high up, hard to reach,
On the top, left-hand shelf of England
Had somehow survived sophistication.

Back in my kitchen I tipped out the five small bricks
And sampled one; nothing special, simple vanilla
And definitely not real cream.
But when I was a boy on a beach
And bought it for fourpence ha'penny
It tasted a treat.

The recipes now are routinely richer,
But in these days of exotic eating
I'd nearly forgotten the first ingredient:
Be hungry!

E L Startin

To See More Clearly

I took my place in the garden of my memories
Where the family played and talked
And laughed together as before.
There were picnics again, and games.
For the moment nobody had fallen over
And the sun was shining on the trees.

I took my seat as bidden by the prayer leader
Somewhere to feel secure and find
That God was present to me
And I to Him
In this hour of stillness
As a psalm was read.

You were all around, remembered in love
As God's unfailing compassion was recalled
For I knew in the depths of my silent spirit
That this had been my privilege and joy
To see the Father's smile
In the eyes of loved ones, family and friends
True soul-companions sharing Heaven's news

The good news that wherever God is found
In this imperfect, waiting, familiar world
Promising paradise hints of things to come
Have taken form between us in the touch
Of hands and voices heard encouraging
To be the best we can, that we are close
Together and to Him.

Thou art in Heaven, we hear; where Heaven is known
Thou art, our Father, day by day more clear.

Christopher Payne

Believing

This event has just gone past
You may not know my name,
Whilst at church on Sunday last
A Christian I became.

I said a prayer of forgiveness
My sins I did repent,
The strain of all the wrong I'd done
Suddenly all went.

Now that I have joined You,
I want to shout aloud,
You have made me feel brand new,
To every single crowd.

I'm sure that I will have some doubt
And times of feeling low,
I know that You will help me out
And all my doubts will go.

I know You'll not desert me
Or ever leave my side.
Thank You Lord, for giving me
This feeling deep inside.

Simon Martin

Swallows

I used to watch when swallows came,
And mark the date, each year,
Because I knew, when they arrived,
That summertime was near.
This year, I did not notice them
Until sometime in May.
They must have been here before then,
But I knew not the day.

One humid day in mid-July
I watched them skimming round,
Swooping down from up on high,
Almost touching the ground,
Teaching their young ones how to fly,
And feeding, as they flew,
They found a plentiful supply
Of airborne insects too!

But now, they fly a different way,
Circling each house and tree,
Repeating flight patterns each day
In one locality.
This imprints on their minds the place
Where they have fed and bred,
So, next year, they their path can trace
To their northern homestead.

Soon, they will mass on cable lines,
Coming from far and near,
Until their inner green light shines,
Giving them their 'all clear'!
Then off they'll go, flight after flight,
One end of summer day.
I'll watch them till they're out of sight,
Sad, that they've gone away.

Nancy Solly

The Tarka Trail Scene

The long grasses form a Mexican wave
Along the side of the Tarka Trail
Nettles, docks and low growing bramble
Fight for space within the crowd.
Foxgloves, iris, dogwood and bindweed
Rise above to show off their special flowers
Whilst the oak, beech, willow and hawthorn
Tower above blown by wind from the sea
And are forever landward bowed.

Joan Earle Broad

Butterflies

Butterflies dancing all in a row
Darting and dashing to and fro,
Up and down and into the trees
Round and round as fast as they please.

The flowers around are a work of art
Which one to pick, where to start?
In each flower they gently dip
Lapping their tongues, the nectar they sip.

Back in the air when they've had their fill
Then fluttering softly over the hill,
Where to go next, what beauty to see?
Look at the rainbow over the trees.

All of nature's a wonderful sight
Something new from morn till night,
When night-time comes, they take a rest
Then rise with the sun full of zest.

Such pretty things are the butterfly
Lovely colours to catch your eye,
Dancing and glistening in the summer sun
Mother Nature's beauty for everyone.

Margaret Anne Hedley

Your Journey's Begun

A long journey lies ahead
I'll make sure you are well fed
Not with just fruits and bread
But with all that I have said
I have furnished you with the tool
So that you will not stand a fool
Although you had a different school
You are acquainted with every rule
So take your leave and go
And to the whole world show
That you did indeed grow
And right from wrong you do know.

Kareen Smith

When Your Children Leave Home

Into your hands, O Lord, I must place
The lives that I love so dear;
No more can I see that they will take care,
But they need to be free, that is clear.

Whatever befalls them, whatever they do,
Lord, may You always be there
To guide them and help them, uplift them and hold them,
The lives that I love so dear.

Janet Moyse

Autumn

I love the autumn days
In very many ways
The lovely colours of the leaves
Falling gently from the trees

The mellow fruit
I love to eat
And fruit to store
For a winter treat

Squirrels are busy too
Storing nuts the way they do
Swallows collect then go away
Hoping to return another day.

I Millington

Just A Reflection For Early September

I see from my kitchen window
Into County Westmeath.
I'm gazing on Mullaghmeen mountain
Now wreathed in autumnal haze.
To the left
The Loughcrew hills
In County Meath so famed,
All this, a pleasant vista
On these autumnal days,
In this
My corner of the world,
Small and yet so fair,
I'm reflecting now
On all God's great world,
Beautiful, majestic,
A world
For all to share.

Brigid Smith

Tell Me

Tell me about your summer friend, did the roses bloom:
the musk and the damask along your path
The creeping sedums in the dark searching
the larkspur bloom of midnight,
before it reached your view, and found its end.

Then to travel on hilly landscapes deep;
the Devonian voice of Watersmeet and Linton's lantern dew
The summer's come and nearly gone, and I should like to know
what woodland path you've trodden, before the winter's snow
Have you seen the jonquils' bloom on the Mendip Hills?

The little menial things that touch, the harebell to the buttercup.
The lispered whispered shaded call of Solomon's seal before the might of Sheba's fall,
Through those Hertford woodlands where we'd kick
The towering, mouldering delves of leaves that smothered all
Our childish dreams; the loudest laughs, that hadn't heard the screams.

Undignified the looking back towards the starting gate,
But my friend, I would like to know about your summer,
When it starts, and where it ends looking for its fate
I would care to know before the shadows overtake,
Choking out the works of art that we enjoyed of late.

R A Toy

Born To Be Free

We are all born into families, for most of us a good, enhancing and beneficial reality. The reality is that everyone has a mum and dad somewhere even brothers and sisters and grandparents. These have passed to us all the emotions, thought processes, intuitions and instincts that make us unique, distinctive personalities. Whatever our circumstances someone has 'been there - done that' and shared somewhat similar reactions to all that is happening. 'There is nothing new under the sun' says the teacher in the book of Ecclesiastes. To every situation with a way in, there is certainly a way out. Looking to God for this way; has given relief to countless individuals over the centuries. Struggle with Him with the issues we face.

God is able and will listen, all we must do for our part is recognise our need for Him - our complete dependence on Him for our substance. God is our friend, the truest friend of all. We can trust Him and confess our need, our total lack of ability to make perfectly sound decisions.

We may feel that life is a particularly small corner, individual as a consequence of our uniqueness. Be unique before our God. He alone knows the beginning from the end. All circumstances come to an end - keep going with hope for the future and also with that particular sure hope in our God. There is nothing you have to tackle that you and He cannot deal with together.

Irene Clare Garner

Looking To The Future

When the bright blue sky clouds over
And day transforms to night,
When a sheet of sapphire covers the top
Another day had passed from sight.

But another day will be created
Who knows what tomorrow will bring?
Who will be our future family?
In a hundred years of wondering

Waiting for time to slowly pass by,
Watching the clock carelessly chime,
When every moment is precious
In this mortal lifetime.

Actions buried deep in the past
Cannot be changed or undone,
In the future wrongs can be made right
To relinquish hurt from someone.

Is it time to make a change?
To spread your wings and fly,
To take to the stars and grab every second
To stop it passing by.

That small child playing on the street
Could soon make our world bright and new,
Because no one really knows what is next
And even the smallest person can surprise you.

The years ahead will soon fly by
Soon we may all live different lives,
In a hopeful world filled with content
Away from all worry and lies.

Just raise a smile to your lips
To make the future happy and true,
To believe in friends, family and others
And to always believe in you.

Bethan Jane Victoria Evans (16)

Untitled

An apple falls from the tree, just for me,
herbs and plants are there for free,
a sheep grows wool from when it's born,
made into a coat to keep me warm.

Who can see? Who can care
for my life here on Earth?

A fish will swim until it's caught
by fearless men who sail the storm.
Would I dare to leave one piece
when this fish died just for me?

Who can see? Who can care
for my life here on Earth?

Fields of gold, fields of wheat
made into bread for us to eat.
A seed is grown from a vine
to multiply a thousand times,
a seed for food, a seed for thought,
these are many treasures sought.

Who can see? Who can care
for my life here on Earth?

Maureen Burleigh

The Beauty Of Creation

I saw the grace of God
In a newborn baby's eyes,
A life so fresh and new,
In need of much tender loving care.

I saw the power of God in the rolling thunder,
In the crashing, tumbling waterfall,
The towering oak tree and the evergreen,
The snow-capped mountains setting the scene.

The beauty of creation is all around to see,
I thank the Lord for His gifts, great and small,
For ears to hear and lips to share
The countless blessings bestowed on us all!

Cathy Mearman

The Light

Where do we seek comfort when the pain is too much to bear?
Where do we seek help to get through the sadness we share?
And where can we find hope again to chase away the despair?

Look for the answer where the light shines bright,
Trust in the love that is never hidden from sight.
Follow the light that you hold in your heart,
For there lies the courage with which to play your part.

Fear not that the light will flicker or fade,
For of heavenly things, this light is made,
Take His hand, let Him lead you, your fears He will release,
And this light will shine and cover the Earth, with rays of hope and peace.

Anne Marie Latham

September Remembered!

*(Dedicated to all those whose lives are ended prematurely
due to the cruel wrongdoing of others)*

I send this out to all who have fallen,
Those who never saw their dreams.
Every good deed I do, I do it for you
And those whose life, was torn at the seams.

Every day that comes round brings us new hope,
Our strength continues to grow.
The daily path of our lives, children and wives
Our love will surely still show.

Never will I forget the list of names,
Those who passed on through this disaster.
I often say, we could reach paradise one day
You arrived there a little bit faster.

Matthew O'Dwyer

The Choice

Put your hand in God's hand as you walk along life's highway
Knowing He will be with you every step of the way

Put your hand in God's hand and you need never fear
Whatever you have to face you can know that He is near

Put your hand in God's hand when you are facing strife
Knowing He will help you to overcome the trials of this life

Put your hand in God's hand, and know you have a friend
Someone who will not forsake you, but will be with you to the end

Put your hand in God's hand when the end is near
His presence will give you the assurance that you long to hear

But, if you are feeling lonely, and you feel all hope is gone
Remember your salvation was bought by the sacrifice of God's son

If you are on your own when your life comes to an end
It's because you have forsaken the one who would be your friend

Assurance or frustration, only you can make the choice
You will make the right one if you listen to His voice

This will bring the message that you long to hear
That whatever you must face you will know that He is near

If you accept His friendship He will be with you to the end
And that is a faithful promise on which you can depend.

Ron Martin

Think Of Me

When the world is on your shoulders,
Think of me . . . I will comfort you.

When the fears come tumbling back,
Think of me . . . I will reassure you.

When you feel lonely, in isolation,
Think of me . . . I will embrace you.

When you're tired, weary of challenge,
Think of me . . . I will rejuvenate you.

When you're scared what may lay ahead,
Think of me . . . I will strengthen you.

When your heart is heavy and unsure,
Think of me . . . I will soothe you.

For I am Love, your love
And love is only a thought away.
Just think of me and I'll be there.

Kay Elizabeth

Reflective Moments

Pause awhile and in the stillness of the moment,
Feel the presence and the power,
As it permeates the spirit,
Energy that moves around and within,
The human form's physical shell,

Breathe the life force,
Which links and unites all creation,
As it bathes us in love, perfect peace and harmony,
We are a part of some divine plan,
A blueprint set into motion from the beginning,

We are but one microscopic dot,
A grain in the canvas of the universe in its entirety,
And yet not insignificant,
For without us the picture would not be complete,
Everything seen and unseen is connected,

From whence the Creator came is a mystery,
Was God in existence before the Alpha
And brought forth the cosmos from a divine ember?
An unknown element that had concept of itself,
Whose creative powers, are beyond man's comprehension,

There is a purpose to us being here,
Perhaps an assessment of the spirit,
As we confront the tribulations we encounter,
Which inevitably give us strength and courage,
This earthly life is but one stage in preparation for the next,

God, a spinning energy of pure light,
At the core of the universe and linked to all in existence,
Our spirits carry the divine spark within,
All of Earth's creations, a miracle that we can witness,
Mysteries to which only the Creator has the answer.

Ann G Wallace

Coral Isle

I found it there a vivid splash
Beset by jewels so rare
The trees were lazy drooping palms
With orchids growing near.

No foot of man had ever trod
Across its sun-kissed face
No architect had ere been there
To spoil its flowered lace.

The sea along its boundaries
Was flecked with white and blue
The sweet hibiscus glaring red
Were soft web spun with dew.

Its cooling fan was nature's breeze
Annexed with salt and spray
Its candlelight a thousand stars
Switched on by close of day.

Its guardian was a yellow moon
Its creed was only give
Its flag a wisp of cloud on high
Its symbol only live.

And as I pondered o'er this sight
The sun began to set
The glory that I saw in her
My mind will ne'er forget.

And as I left my coral isle
To wander o'er the blue
I stood to watch it fade from sight
And bid it sweet adieu.

G W Hubbard

Keeping Faith

When darkness falls and daylight ceases,
Rest assured you are in safe keeping.
Through channels of your dreamlike sleep, increases
Your feelings of drifting, towards a Heaven unknown, while sleeping.

Every dawn that starts a brand new day,
Is in keeping with the Creator's ultimate plan.
To believe blindly, one would say,
Is a test of faith, without compromise, for man.

When troubles fall upon your shoulders,
And keeping faith is hard to do,
Take your problems to the Lord who holds you -
In your life, not just now, but all the way through.

Hold on to faith - when feeling lost,
For the Lord counts all His sheep.
He is the shepherd, who, at any cost,
Will find you peace, calm, and joy to keep.

Though the burden of life can be heavy,
And the way through, impossible to find,
Keeping faith with the Lord will assist you -
He will help you to attain peace of mind.

If you are weary, and feeling downtrodden,
And life seems too much to bear,
Take your prayers to the Lord who will hear them,
Keeping faith with Him who cares.

Hilarie Grinnell

Harvest Time

Praise God for
Harvest time again
His bounty towards us
Will surely remain
He stands by His promise
That while Earth
Shall be
His provision continues
To you and to me.
Such generosity
Is beyond compare
Let us kneel
Before Him
In humble prayer.
As our hearts
We raise
In grateful praise
Let not be forgot
Those who have not.

P A Fazackarley

God Knows And Cares

In a town in the world,
  In the park in that town,
    At a spot in that park,
      A sparrow fell down,
      And God knew.

In a town in the State 34,
  Near Route 29 in a shed,
    Lives a poor man, aged 61
      With 8,000 hairs on his head.
      Which God knows.

In a field in the country,
  In a rich, loamy soil,
    Grows a beautiful lily
      Without sweat or toil.
      As God knows.

You think God does not see,
  And at times does not care,
    But He sees the sparrow falling
      And can number your hair.
    The lily in its beauty
      He grows with no strife.
        So rest in God's love,
        He cares for your life.
God knows.

Colin Wide

Happiness Is . . .

Happiness is like seeing a rainbow in the sky
Watching a new life come into the world
Feeling the drops of a summer rain shower as you dance to its tune
Or the warmth of the sun on your skin.

Happiness comes from the thoughts that you think
Giving you the warm feeling inside
That spreads throughout your entire body
And reaches to the outside to put a smile on your face.

Happiness is something that we can share with others
When you give someone flowers and see the smile appear on their face
To help others that are less fortunate
By finding the simplest things that surround us and share them around.

Happiness is all around us
We just have to let ourselves feel it
If you believe in happiness and are positive
Happiness will always be part of your life.

Julie Banyard

Simply Wonderful

Crock of gold at the end of the rainbow
In a place near the river
Silver-haired lady so shady
Melting moments surround us

Crack in the wall so tall
Figure of fun just one
Never say never
Always remember your manners

Tell like it is
Leave nothing out
Imaginative flights of fancy
Simply wonderful darling, simply wonderful.

S M Thompson

Daily Reflections

Trust

I must face up to my
Innermost thoughts
As things go round
In my head
To try and discover
What I really want
After what others have said
I try to interpret what
Matters to them
But they all have individual minds
I have come to a crossroad
That no one can help
Because I am the one who decides
I think I will let time
Escape for a while
And see what my prayers will bring
To trust in the Lord
Is a wonderful thing

Mary Tickle

A Bird In The Hand

Wandering through the garden,
How the soil had hardened,
Praying for a sign of rain,
Plants would relish a shower again.

My vision travelled and came to rest,
Baby green finch, feathers glistening upon his chest.
His stance remained composed, relaxed,
Sudden alarm he'd fly away, a well known fact.

Stretching my hand, my voice a soft whisper,
Reaching fingers closed, a warm, feathered listener.
Here in my hand, just a moment in time,
Esteem valued offering, trusting response, God's gift to mankind.

Pausing an instant, then decided to fly,
A memory cherished, with a comforting sigh.
A garden is a paradise, where nature's gifts surround,
Each season brings God's oblations, often rich in sound.

Lorna Tippett

Lorna Tippett

The Circle

God's love is a circle, pure gossamer threads,
Gentle strength that cannot be broken,
It's made up of hearts who answered His call,
The step of repentance taken,

Come enter God's circle it widens with love,
Circumference forever increasing,
A mighty throng searching for peace,
The hungry, the lame, the weeping,

Jesus beckons to all, His arms open wide,
For your dear sakes please answer His call,
Then God's circle of love will encompass the world,
And Satan's regime will fall.

Dorothy M Mitchell

Jesus, My Best Friend

My best friend is Jesus; He's with me everywhere,
though I cannot see Him, I know He's in the very air.
I see Him in the colours, of flowers, birds and trees.
I hear Him in the water's flow, the wind, the gentle breeze.
When I am down He comforts me, His arm round me is strong.
When I am tempted from the path, He shows me where I am wrong.
When I laugh, I feel Him smiling, like a warming glow inside.
If sad, I know He's crying, His sorrow He can't hide.
Any time that I am lonely I can go, walk and talk, with Him,
or sit and quietly listen, I hear Him, deep within.
He's there in all my labours; He tries to take my load,
as He did, for all our sakes, when He staggered up the road,
that led Him finally, to His death, carrying a cross of wood,
which represented all our sins, this He understood.
Yes, He'll take my burden; He will carry yours as well,
to keep you safe, away from harm, He'll stand, twixt you and Hell.
My best friend is Jesus; He would be your friend too,
just ask, I'll introduce you. I'll show Him to you.

Brian Muchmore

My Faith

It seems it's common now to view
My faith as a childish toy retained
As sentimental trophy from
A golden past that never was.
They're unaware this anchor rope
Has held me true through tempest blasts.
At times it broke a fall that left
Me dangling by a shelf above
A dizzy drop to gorge below.
Regaining safety's ledge, it's helped
To link me in a chain of love
To fellow pilgrims climbing track
That leads to kingdom Christ proclaims.
I claim my rope of faith is steel,
A trusted guide to all that's real.

Henry Disney

Everyday Wonders

I sit in the silence,
the peace and the calm,
I am thankful for this day,
the rising of the dawn.
I soak up the splendour
of God's great light,
and behold this day,
as it takes over the night . . .
I muse over miracles
that unfold before my eyes,
the singing of the birds,
the flowers in disguise . . .
To think of all that God has created
on this Earth for us to see,
all that could bring peace,
love and harmony . . .
If only we are willing,
to learn to let things go,
to look within our hearts,
we would find what we need to know . . .
To learn to take a moment
to slow down in our day,
we could find our balance within
and hear what spirit has to say . . .
I am so grateful
for what this day will hold,
so much in store for me,
everyday wonders, more precious than gold . . .

Kitty Morgan

Have Faith In God

I know you've tramped many a stony road
And climbed many a punishing hill
And throughout those years you carried your load
And succeeded, because of your 'will'.

The road that you find yourself following now
Must seem steeper and quite without end
And I'm certain you must be wondering how
Without help, you will get round the bend.

But remember the stiles and the ridges you climbed
And the woods that seemed endless and dense,
Remember the birdsong, the church bells that chimed
When, emerging, you'd rest by a fence.

Each hour of each day is a new stile to climb
Each week, a new pathway to plod
But birds are still singing and church bells still chime
And you'll win if you have faith in God.

For He is the friend who will carry your load,
His strength and His love are unfailing,
Keep Him by your side as you travel the road
And the journey you'll find is plain sailing.

Eileen Martin

Autumn

The end of a beautiful autumn day,
The setting sun casting a golden glow
Over trees everywhere,
O Sovereign Lord, O Great Creator,
No man can paint a picture
Such as this!

A canvas of brilliant grandeur,
Rustic charm and peaceful emotion.
'I am the Lord, I change not!'
Yes Father this scene portrays that fact –
Season follows season as night follows day,
Great is Your faithfulness.

Open our eyes to recognise Your handiwork,
To see Your glory and acknowledge Your goodness.
What is man that You are mindful of him?
Indeed Lord we are undeserving
Of all the good that comes from Your hand.
Yet in Your love You pour out blessing upon blessing
In humble gratitude we receive from You
Including the breathtaking sight
Of Your world bathed in autumn glory.

Mary Davies

Parenthood

At the end of a challenging day
When she's tucked up in bed, we can smile
Watching over our Sleeping Beauty
We realise it's all been worthwhile.

A little rascal by day
An angel by night
We kiss her velvet soft cheek
Then turn out the light.

Penelope Collinson

The Greatest Love

To be loved by the Lord and to love Him too
Is the greatest joy that can happen to you.
As all through your life this blessing will grow
And your days will be bright in its wonderful glow.
The strength of the Lord is all that we need
To help us in every thought, word and deed.
When life storms threaten and faith isn't strong,
Trust in the Lord as you travel along,
And when your grey skies turn into blue,
It's the love of the Lord that is seeing you through.
So tender His comfort in all of His ways,
His love in abundance to bless all our days.

O gracious Lord, You're the One we adore,
Remain in our hearts for evermore.

Enid Rathbone

Daily Reflections

School Gates

September is upon us again,
Children nervously wait at school gates,
Anticipation, excitement, thrill,
But wanting to cling to Mum still,
Four years old and full of fun,
An era has ended, a new one begun,
Mum's feelings are very mixed too,
Pride, doubts, misgivings, to mention a few,
Gran, shares these as with younger brother she stays,
Wonders what has happened to all the days,
Since her first grandson, she held in her arms,
As the younger child she now calms,
She looks forward to viewing the school play,
And of course, October, and the first school holiday.

Nita Roskilly

Wave-Waltzing With Lymphoma

The day I had cancer was quite a surprise
With its earlier symptoms hid from my eyes
But the hospital scanning removed any doubt.
An exciting new prospect, as I soon found out.

When faced with a life-change as solemn as this
There are parts of our life that we don't want to miss
But the truth must be faced and there's nowhere to hide
And the treatment sure sounds like a roller-coast ride.

How long have I got, is the question in mind
As I reach out for someone I know to be kind.
He tells me I need now to banish all fear
Throughout chemotherapy He will be near.

My days are all numbered, I won't miss a day
So should use every one, not let them fritter away.
'I'm in charge of your care. You are in my employ.
I will give you my peace and will fill you with joy.'

All of these promises prove to be true
For He is as loving to me as to you.
It's something we need to not ever forget,
For what's still to come will then be the best yet.

If you've surfed a big wave, felt its terminal drive
Felt its power and its weight, you're so keenly alive.
How long the ride lasts, from beginning to end
As you land on the shore there awaits still your friend.

Though the taste in my mouth is both salty and sweet
To bless and encourage the people I meet,
When grounded at last at the end of the fun
I will surely look forward to meeting the Son.

John Foster-Turner

The Lamb

No parting or approaching night,
Just dawn of unimagined light.
Within The Lamb's high dwelling place,
Among the meadowlands of space.

There sits The Lamb upon His throne,
With laughter in His blessed bones.
A crown of lilies on His brow,
Such marvel does the time allow.

Ten thousand, thousands praises bring,
As round His throne the angels sing
In blossom-bursting harmony
Worthy The Lamb, all glory be.

Idris Woodfield

Beautiful Autumn

I wonder why the dear Lord made Autumn
The most beautiful season of them all?
The time when plump fruits and red berries come
To load trees before their russet leaves fall.
Crisp Autumn is a time of fulfilment,
Harvest shows the dear Lord has blessed the seed,
Soft spring rain and summer sunshine, He sent
To provide fruits of the earth that we need.
As crisply bronzed leaves swirl onto the soil,
Little creatures harvest their winter store,
And men look for rest after summer toil,
On long sunny days, having closed the door.
But in such beauty in fall and decay,
God promises rebirth in Spring's new days!

Pat Heppel

Solace In Stillness

Cattle slowly amble in the open fields,
unknowing of what is in store for them alone.
The present is enough, with luscious grass available -
out in the warming sun and cooling rain.
Passers-by pause to look at animal faces gazing languidly
over the stone wall,
Their long tongues curled round new bramble shoots.

The world's Creator makes provision for everyone.
The human need to love and care for others,
the physical need to live a valuable and worthwhile life,
the social need for friends and family,
and like the cattle look on their farmer to guide, protect and nurture,
our spiritual need for dependent trust in an unfailing God.

'He owns the cattle on a thousand hills',
the harvest hymn-writer tells us graphically.
His arms outstretched to enfold the believer, means
we are forever in the family of God.
All the heartaches, pains and misunderstandings of life are covered
by the everlasting promises of our Heavenly Father's grace.

When the world seems to have gone crazy
and we disagree with decisions made by those set over us,
it is heartening to remember that nobody can take away our thoughts
nor our beliefs, the very citadel of our personality.
And our omnipotent, loving God is in control, who in the end
will reign over us in the glory of peace, where
'the lion shall lie down with the lamb'.

A Audrey Agnew

Never Give Up Searching

Jesus sends this message
To let you know He hears
To let you know He's feeling
All your hopes and fears

He hears you when you're crying
And He sees you when you're sad
He's with you when you're lonely
Arms of love you've never had

It breaks His heart to see you
Trying to bear the pain
Give all your troubles up to God
So you're free to live again

He wants to bear your burdens
And He'll keep them up above
So that you are free to welcome
His gifts of peace and love

He chose you for a reason
He sees all you've got to give
His light will guide you onwards
To the life you long to live

He knows your path's been rocky
But now your seed's been sown
He'll help you find the love
And the joy you've never known

Jesus is the water
That will bring your seed along
And Jesus is the sunshine
That will keep you ever strong

And Jesus sends this message
He'll promise life anew
So never give up searching
Because He's out there searching too

Lesley Heath

2nd October

Precious Memories

Time moves on with wonderful memories to share
Beautiful feelings that stemmed from a precious love enfolding
As I take in just how these changes have taken place
I realise the sun has shone on me with the beauty of everlasting love.

Everyday pleasurable times contrast with memories of the distant past
I really appreciate just how love entered my life
Better times came with the completion of a special relationship
Marriage brought about an avalanche of exceptional happiness

Dreams increase creativity with beautiful feelings to share
Pride and acceptance of individuality builds upon trust
Today love brings hope and ultimate fulfilment
Precious memories are to be treasured and never forgotten.

Marjory Price

Creator King

Heavenly Father, merciful King
Creator of always and everything
You hear my words before they are said
Have counted the hairs on this humble head

Eternal God, patient teacher
Giver of past, present and future
Provider of light in my darkest hour
My life exists because of Your power

Sharon Brewer

Sunshine

Every ray of sunshine brings a ray of hope,
It fills your heart with joy, enables you to cope.
The warm sun on your face, hot sand under your feet,
A piece of chocolate in your mouth is certainly a treat.
Waking in the morning, and hearing the birds sing,
Light streaming through the window, what will the new day bring?
A warm smile from a stranger in the shopping street,
Makes it worth the heavy bags, and the blistered feet.
The homely smell of cooking as you walk through the door,
A cuddle from a loved one is enough to reassure.
A delicate new flower, with its vibrant coloured bloom,
Its scent drifting on the breeze, banishes the gloom.
An appealing furry kitten, meowing for her food,
Is enough to fill you with love and lift a sagging mood.
A little dimpled baby, his life about to start,
His little smiles and gurgles surely melt the heart.
A roaring fire blazing on a cold winter's night,
The snowflakes fluttering down outside are such a pretty sight.
Celebrating Christmas, with those that you hold dear.
Just a few examples of the treasures found each year.

Julie Wealleans

A Brand New Day

I wake up each morning to a brand new day
And I thank the Lord and what can I say?
Thank you for the Earth and the sky,
The birds of the air as they wing by,
The squirrel trying to find his store
Of goodies he buried that he can't remember where!
The blue tit flying up and down
To feed her fledglings' gaping yawn.
I can see a snail who moves not at all,
Perhaps he's still asleep and ignores the morning's call,
To get up and live, there's a new day to explore,
The sun's getting higher and what is more
I've just realised it's my day off today,
Shall I go back to bed? I've had my say.
No! I'm up and glad to be alive
And anyway, eight hours sleep should help me survive!
So what shall I do? Go for a walk
Along the seashore and forget all of this talk.
I've said my thanks to you know who!
So I'll just enjoy my day, how about you?

R Bateman

Today

You've opened your eyes to see the morning light
Another new day has begun after the night
Yesterday's happenings are gone – just a memory
What will today bring? Just wait and see.

Life is wonderful, there's so much to do
The sun's rays are just coming into view
Nature is magic, a garden full of flowers
Trees full of birds sing their songs for hours.

Sky full of wonder, white clouds moving by
Sun, moon and stars way up high
Oh yes it's a wonderful world, enjoy while you may
This is the start of a beautiful day.

Ethel Wakeford

A Gift

The greatest gift of all
Is that of being given
The 'gift of life'.

And the second greatest gift
Is that of appreciating
That of which you've been given.

And being of the wish –
To share –
Likewise, with all others
Given the same.

Bakewell Burt

Marriage

Marriage is a symbol,
a gift from up above.
A sign of your commitment,
a display of all your love.
Marriage is a partnership,
designed to give and take.
Sharing with one another,
a happy home you'll make.
Marriage is forever,
remember that from the start.
Love and care for one another,
with feelings shown from the heart.
Marriage joins two soulmates,
to enjoy the rest of their life.
It binds the two together,
from now on, husband and wife.

Helen Rees-Smith

Life

If Life were but a question
Would you answer with the truth?
With all the things you ever did
Right back to your youth?

If Life was but a challenge
Would you rise above it all?
Would you face it with a smile
Or break and crumble, then fall?

If Life was but a path
Would you find your way?
Would you follow the hills up and down
Or would you go astray?

If Life was but a test
To find your inner soul
Would you find a cave of treasure
Or just an empty hole?

Shelley Parker

This beautiful June morning
prompts special memories
twelve months ago this very day
in that church between the trees
we stood together arm-in-arm
I nearly choked with pride
the day darling you honoured me
and became my blushing bride.

I never thought life held for me
such joy, such bliss, such hope,
my whole life changed that blessed day
before - how did I cope?
Best friend and lover both you've proved
you really are my rock
I count the minutes, hours, days
then pinch myself in shock.

Please God shine down Your face on us
and grant that this will last
not forever, of course it can't
for time-space is so vast
and we who merely mortals be
must one day turn to dust
and then depart this mortal coil
farewell this earthly crust.

Lord grant then when we soar above
into Your spiritual home
that we might remain hand-in-hand
whilst paradise we roam.

George Jones

A Calling To Dance!

Life is a dance!
Take each step lightly,
For you are so small in the vastness of it all!
Listen to the life inside your own body.
Feel it calling you like a sweet melody.

When you feel alone,
Reach out from the cold
And touch someone's soul.
We all need love, you know.
Talk with the trees, the flowers, the bees,
Listen to life,
And the voice in the breeze.

Look at the sky and the clouds passing by.
Tell me, why do you sigh,
When you can skip, leap . . . and fly!

Dance, dance, just *dance* with life,
Your most intimate lover,
From which you can't hide.
Dance with the fears,
Dance with the pain.
Don't run away.
They'll only come back again.

Dance, dance,
Embrace all that you be.
The darkness will fall away
And then you will see
That life is for loving,
So let your heart sing,
For you are the life that's within everything!

Hannah Cullingford

Hidden Treasure

In desolate places, or dark secret mine
There may be some 'treasure' that has lasted through time
Hidden deep down 'neath the gaze of today
Its value unknown to those passing that way

Within a 'shy' person there may be much we don't see
Hidden values unknown to you and to me
Talents worth having - a character fine
That shouldn't be hidden to stagnate all the time

Let's find and draw out these people's good gifts
Help each reach potential - give them some 'lifts'
When unobtrusively helping according to need
You may help yourself too - and show friendship indeed.

Muriel I Tate

To The Lords I Pray

To the lord of the morning,
To the lord of the day,
To the lord of the evening,
To the Lord I pray.

At the start of the morn,
When the dark fades away,
Sweet birds will sing,
Praising each day
To the lord of the morning,
To the Lord I pray.

As the day comes alive,
With laughter and life,
Our balance of nature
Just feels to be right,
To the lord of the day,
To the Lord I pray.

At the end of the day,
The moon crowns the dark,
All things come to rest,
Before a new start,
To the lord of the evening,
To the Lord I pray.

To the lord of the morning,
To the lord of the day,
To the lord of the evening,
To the Lord I pray.

A Creighton

Untitled

Some people seem to think
That happiness can be bought,
Such sentiment is misleading
And with danger is fraught.
Contentment of mind is true wealth
And that can never ever be bought,
But the means of achieving it
Can sometimes be taught.
Try to spread a little sunshine
As you go along your way.
Show love and compassion to others
Throughout each live-long day.
You will find your spirits rising
In just a very little while,
For nothing is as infectious
As a warm and loving smile.

Robert H Quin

God Paints A Beautiful Picture

God painted a beautiful picture
In colours of every hue
In a myriad of textures
He created a wonderful view

God painted a beautiful picture
The universe and all that it holds
Created for his own pleasure
Magnificent, majestic and bold

God painted a beautiful picture
An infant so perfect and sweet
The best loved of all his creations
His masterpiece was complete

God painted a beautiful picture
And into it his own spirit blew
And life sprang forth from his drawing
Giving breath to all that he drew

God painted a beautiful picture
Which he loved from that very first dawn
And he offered life eternal
To all who could see what he'd drawn

Denise Tidswell

Autumn Leaves

Dancing and twisting so graceful and slow
Tracing their spirals in the cool breeze,
Autumn leaves falling, tango to and fro
Celebrating freedom from parkland trees.
They jostle each other in sensuous swirls
Catching the sunlight and chasing a gust,
Then, down to the ground with flamboyant twirls -
A final bow before turning to dust.
In fiery bronzes and all shades of red,
With silver, gold and the deepest of brown,
Earth paints for our pleasure her soft leaf bed,
God's created glory, earth's fallen crown.
But lovers out walking just do not see
And children in scarves wreck leaf-piles with glee.

David Radford

Rain

Why did the raindrop come down from the sky?
Did it fall? Overflow?
Was it sent with a mission?

Was the raindrop reluctant
To leave where it was
Happily sailing as part of a cloud?

Was the raindrop unconscious
Of all that transpired
On the dry and drying crust of the earth?

Or was the raindrop waiting the moment
Ready and willing to give up its life
To be life-giving drink for the thirsty land?

Whatever the reason, it came in profusion,
One drop not enough, it poured and poured,
Wherever it landed the earth was transformed:

Barren ground burst forth in profusion of growth
Colour and perfume became its response
And the trees were laden with fruit.

Oonagh Twomey

Angel . . .

A sketchy array of colours,
A canvas of black and white,
Wild shadows circulate,
It's half-past ten at night.
    I'm trying to write a poem,
Bold air rushes through the trees,
I cannot concentrate though -
Whilst-you-are-watching-me.
    Shadows of the night caress my weary skin,
Disharmony disrupts the room,
Angel . . . you may come in.
    A silver spectrum of the room,
Illuminates an empty space,
No cliché wings or halo,
Just a warm consoling face
    Raindrops embrace my window,
An insecure softness corrupts the room,
With hesitant eyes I ponder,
As your presence slowly moves.
    Such a brief supreme encounter,
Though the atmosphere ceases to calm,
A darkness like no other,
I know you meant no harm.
    Angel? Can you hear me?
Angel - if you're there,
Thank you for your guidance -
Your warmth, love and care.

Laura H Powell

Music

Music speaks volumes without e'er a word,
A language understood by all nations when in an ear heard,
Even a newborn babe in a mother's arm
Recognises the lullaby hummed softly to make calm.
Music has the gift of lifting from the depths of despair
And can soothe away the sorrow when it is there to share,
It needs no words to sense the mood it's in,
With the highs and the lows paints a picture from within.
The music of the Bible, some of which David wrote
Are so beautiful when on wings of music float.
The 23rd Psalm, loved by all and which we all know
Has such depth of meaning, when set to music makes the tears to flow.
The church organ thunders out notes deeply resonant to reach the soul,
Yet some are sweet and mellow to feel His presence, to feel once more whole.
That's when without reason it sends ripples down the spine
Making a sound of music so heavenly and divine.
It is a God-given gift, so let us our voices raise
As in prayers of thankfulness we lovingly sing His praise.
Music is the food of love, so said, and love makes the world go round
So for peace the world over, let love in music resound.

Tess Walton

Today

One day, each day at a time,
This is all I've had to focus on.
- Just recently -
Just for the now,
Each daily hour.
Look up to the sky,
For me, with an artist's eye.
Blues, pinks, yellows, white,
A rainbow feint.
The light from the sky,
Shining off buildings high.
The days turned from night,
A promise in the rainbow
That God is faithful.
Today, tomorrow - the future
My God knows.
But for me, each day
Each hour that comes
Is enough to think about
Till tomorrow comes.
I look to the sky,
Today it's grey,
With an artist's eye.
But I know it may,
Change throughout the day.
Light shining through a shower,
Taking me on hour by hour.
That's enough for me
I don't need a whole picture to see today.

Val Connolly

My Accident, 1994

When I was crippled at the time
A friend of mine came into mind
'Who can I ask for help?' I said
When I lay helplessly in my bed
'I'll help,' a friend replied, as I lay helpless and denied
'Thank God,' I said, in great demand as he came
To my side and held my hand
Without him I could not have existed
Thank God my particular path was listed
'Have faith in me,' he replied
And slowly faded from my side
I knew then from that very day
That my Lord was with me in every way.

Bob Lowe

Spirit, Spirit, Rest In Me

Spirit, spirit, rest in me,
Take me in your embrace,
Holy spirit, dwell in me
Fill my heart with your grace.

Spirit, spirit, take my mind,
Cleanse it and free it from sin
Teach me what forgiveness is,
And fill me with love within.

Spirit, spirit, come to me,
Change me so I can be
Just like Jesus Christ Our Lord,
From now to eternity.

Spirit, spirit, fill my soul
With compassion and faith in thee,
Holy spirit be my guide
In all that I try to be.

Spirit, spirit, from on high
You're special and dear to me,
Please holy spirit as I pray to you
Come and dwell in me.

George T Terry

Autumn Delights

Days of bright sunlight or,
mists damp, drifting, silent.
Flowers give up their blossom
as chill nights steal them away.
Brown polished conkers shiny, round,
lie hiding next to the acorns,
their caps on the ground.
Hands reach for the biggest,
a winner of contest,
the very best to be found.
Clouds crawl across the sky,
smoky old bonfires,
watering eye Catherine wheels,
rockets, gunpowder plot.
Potatoes in their jackets still hot.
The Earth sighs, then slumbers
till it's time to begin
the magic of spring.

Joy Hubbard

Untitled

Just one hour in the day
Can change our lives –
Sad news, bad news
May alter minds.
At the end of that day
You may give a sigh,
Not knowing how
You got through the time.

Someone was guiding me,
Someone was there,
Giving me strength,
Holding me where
I was weak and fearful,
Lost and alone –
This was a god
I have never known,
Loving, tender,
Supportive too –
It took a bad day
To get close to you.

Marjorie Dobbs

Untitled

When you're feeling down and a little low
Smile and let the warmth inside you glow
At times like these think of me
Think of all the good things, think of Rhi
Step outside and breathe the air
You are in my thoughts, I am always there
Remember what makes you laugh and smile
Sit down and enjoy those things for a while
Above all remember this thing
My love is everlasting

Gareth Fontaine

A Prayer For A New Day

Dear God,
A simple prayer to You I pray,
Be by my side throughout the day,
And may all the things I say or do
Reflect the love that comes from You.
Where there's despair, pray, bring me hope,
When I feel weak, please help me cope,
And when I feel my anger burn,
May it be to You I turn.
And when the cold, dark night appears,
Relieve me Lord of all my fears,
Forgive me Lord of all my sins
Until another day begins . . .

Kevin Baskin

The Flower

I hadn't kept her long
But I kept her safe
I found her a nice little spot
In a sunny place

She sat on the window sill
Ready to bud
Into an illumination of coloured floods

I watched in awe as every detail blossomed
Out from her leaves
An array of delicate petals
That were so pleasing to see

She had the sweetest scent
When the bees suckled
From the heavens sent

Who would have thought
A flower could give
So much pleasure
And appreciation

Just shows we can have a tiny piece of beauty
Without having to cause damnation

Emma Bacon

Some Nights

There are some nights
that have to be
endured alone.

No one else
can pace the floor for you.
No one else
can find the dawn
on your behalf.

Such is your lot,
child of Adam.
In the terrible dark of it,
there is no one else there
to share the knowledge,
to allay the guilt
or to quieten the fears.

And always,
in the terrible dark of it,
there is the struggle
to keep alive
a memory
of the calming cosmic voice.

Yet, in this night,
strange as it seems,
we are - all of us -
still more than halfway
to paradise.

Stephen Eric Smyth

Autumn

The chestnut trees in autumn dress
Dominate the skyline. Beneath,
Pavements become rich carpets spread
With tawny leaves, or a gold wreath

In memory of summer days
Now ended for another year.
I like the autumn best of all,
When squirrels hunt for nuts, and peer

From halfway up a tree trunk as
We pass; and children, just like we
Did, long ago, search in the grass
For conkers. Yet I cannot see

The autumn come without regret;
Remembering how he loved to see
Tawny chrysanthemums and leaves
Blazing like fire in some old tree.

Dorothy Davis-Sellick

Daily Reflections

The Golden Smile

Every day's a good day, valued more than wealth;
Be grateful to what gods there be, if you are blessed with health;
All of us have problems, until the final bell;
It's only our reaction, which makes it heaven or hell.

We should be thankful for our senses, which give us such delight,
To smell and taste and feel, and the eyes which give us sight,
The hands and magic fingers, with which we work or play,
Will pat a baby's back, or clasp for us to pray.

Excessive money's worthless, if you gamble it for health,
A level of contentment is greater far than wealth;
Look for a happy face, as you travel out today,
It shines out like a beacon light, showing you the way.

I've travelled round the world, seen people of all creeds,
Some have been important and carried out great deeds;
But the people I remember, from the Tiber to the Nile,
Had glorious golden faces, which gave to me, a smile.

John Hanner

Leap Year

There's so much I can't explain:
Not just the practical things
Like how a steam train works
Or the off side rule,
But answers I can't find at the library –
Why the doorbell rings as soon as you sit on the toilet
Or someone telephones just when you're thinking about them.

Then there's the emotions (not just my age!):
When I've thought my heart was breaking
It never has, quite,
When decisions were beyond me
There's always been a nudge,
And when I haven't wanted to go on
I've realised that someone needed me.

This year there will be 366 chances to get things right,
An extra day to do better,
And to put others first.

It isn't selfish to want to be happy –
Just difficult to see how it's done:
We travel hopefully on a materialistic road
Yet it's beauty and music that stir the tears.

Take joy to someone else,
Forgive and try to forget,
And trust that whatever happens is for the best.

I can't explain it, but it works for me.

Barbara Newman

27th October

Faith

You touched my heart on meeting as I looked in your eyes
And I could see all kinds of things much to my surprise,
I saw the understanding of many people's needs,
I saw the act of giving the many mouths to feed,
I also saw the sadness and the silent tears that fell,
And I could see the love but you couldn't tell,
Red satin all around you and jewels in your hair,
I also see white lilies strewn everywhere,
Your heart is big and bold, your feelings sincere,
But you can't solve the problems of all the people here,
People lost forever, never coming home,
Parents waiting silently by the telephone,
Hush don't cry I hear you say tomorrow is another day,
There may be loved ones oh so near,
Trust in the Lord I hear you say,
For our good news may come today.

Ellen Chambers

Humble

Simple and clear
it was always so
bread and cheese
some water from the spring
due attention paid
to daily tasks
beeswax for the candle
a quill
as white as snow
the sanctity
of the everyday
life lived
on the western edge
eyes straining searching
creating works of loveliness
for our Lord

Look at it
and do not turn away
though it will burn
and scorch you
the transmutation of base elements
to something finer
the true image
behind the false
the eternal surge
of the ocean
in your ears
for God will hold you
in His palm forever

Julian Ronay

The Timeless Moment

In a dream-like state now came this vision:
It was morning and daylight, not yet fully conscious,
Content to prolong sensation of drifting effortlessly
And savouring the varied visions conjured from within.
Staring out of the window, not seeing what was there,
But, rather, of beyond.

In a moment, a multitude of people passed
Who were of great influence on my life for some phase,
As events from the past unfurled before my inward eye
A lifetime's experience was recreated in that instant,
The rich tapestry of life embedded in the subconscious
Now vividly revealed.

As the mystery of life gradually unfolded,
Of birth, childhood, procreation, middle age, old age,
Came the knowledge now that to understand every stage,
As the seasons, was to understand life's truth itself;
In this state, when past, present and future are one,
A wholeness was seen.

Through religion, philosophy and art,
Many are the paths that lead to that inner peace;
Lingering quietly, in the realm of the spirit,
Where there is no separation between soul and flesh,
Then inspiration in all that is beautiful emerges
Through eyes open at last.

Betty Mealand

Special Angel

When darkness comes to fill your days
Heart weighted down beneath its load
And reasons why just can't be found
Although you've searched the endless road.
Do not let your soul be sad
Do not dwell within despair
Though you may feel you stand alone
The world around appears unfair.

There is light beyond the hilltops
Growing brighter with each dawn
Let your face bathe in its glory
Allow His love to keep you warm
Take the hand of your special angel
He walks with you in whispered prayer
Allow His peace to fill your heart
While He keeps you safe within His care.

Elizabeth Bowes

The Peace Within

Everybody's different,
Different likes and different ways,
But for each of us there is
A special person, time or place.

For some it's sitting in a church,
Always quiet and serene,
For others, walking in the woods
Or garden, somewhere green.

For some it's listening to birds,
Or hearing a baby laugh,
And some people find their inner self
Relaxing in the bath.

Whatever turns you on is good
As long as it's no sin
For everybody needs that peace
You only find within.

Diana Price

Friendship

There comes a time
When you look back
And there are certain things
That keep appearing
Memories will never be forgotten
Memories are what form life.

Then there is something that goes deeper
That is the bond between two
A relationship has started
And a friendship has begun.

Friends will laugh and cry
Love and hate
But the bond will never be broken
When you move on to new things
Moving home
Changing jobs
Starting a family
Look back and smile.

Take the memories with you
But take your friendship further
When you have built that bond
Never be afraid of what's yet to come
You know you will never be alone.

Sharon Atkinson

1st November

The Darkening Days

The alluring winter sun is setting;
an orange ball, throwing her amber rays
far reaching, soul searching,
a promise to the viewer of better days.

Salmon pink linings under each darkened cloud;
radiant energy in every beam of light.
Entranced by such beauty, I gaze in awe,
stark silhouettes cast as she sinks from sight.

The splendour of this vision fills my soul
with a desire to follow the ethereal light,
to banish the coldness, distress and the fear
of the darkening days,
though salvation is near.

Tracey Lynn Birchall

Rainbow

I rode the rainbow in search of me,
Dazzled by the spectrum of life's complexity.
I climbed the arc and when I reached the top
I could survey the red of my success, the violet of my flops,
The yellow of laughter and the blue of tears,
Each colour touched my soul, settled in my brain
Wiping away the monochrome of inexperience and fears,
But something lacked I knew
Until I slid back to earth again
To find my pot of gold was you.

Robert Peirce

The Fish Are Swimming

The fish are swimming in the brook
On this sunny day,
As one may look,
Glitter, glitter the water shines,
Just like this very day,
For God has made it so fine,
And all around there is countryside,
Which gives this setting.
The wonder of a heavenly time,
So look, look on and you will find,
There is nothing wrong,
For all of magic of our time,
Really does make these glittering ways,
A definite sign, yes the fish are swimming,
In this very picturesque brook,
The sun is shining on this day
And there are bullrushes growing
Up from the edge,
Just to make the sight of these waters,
The sight of Heaven which is
Shining all of each day.

C Hush

String Of Pearls

Life is a collection of moments,
A beautiful string of pearls.
No money is needed to buy these.
They are not presents from princes and earls.
It's the smile of a stranger in passing;
The first time your child calls you, 'Mum';
Or the little chirp on your window;
Golden rays from the setting sun.
Sometimes there may be a black pearl,
Said to be the most precious of all;
For me, these were words from my husband,
While waiting for the final call.
Words in the form of a question,
Though frequently spoken still true;
Let me share with you my precious black pearl:
'When last did I tell you I loved you?'

Helga Dharmpaul

Something Else

Out there is something else;
Why don't you leave your cage -
Engage your mind
In matters more profound?
Be still and you may hear
A whisper in the wind
Or feel an angel's wing caress your hair:
If you are quiet enough you'll find
That something else that waits for us
Out there.

Leo Taylor

Jilligoon Park

With peace and tranquillity sitting beside me
And the lake of serenity's stillness right by
We'd sit and devour the first taste of morning
And then for desserts there's a strawberry sky.

This deafening silence embraces each moment
And keeps me transfixed on the unfolding scene
With night-time departing and the daylight arriving
And the gathering of colours with stars in between.

The angelic glow that emits from its splendour
Generates calmness with its comforting shine
Propelling all woes to another dimension
Allowing the body and soul to unwind.

This celestial portrait on its heavenly easel
Stirs the emotions and stimulates minds
While pulling you close in a mesmerised vacuum
Leaving all logic and reason behind.

You can keep all your Turners and Monets and Renoirs
Your Salvador Dalis and Vincent Van Goghs
Just sit down with me at the break of the dawning
And there we'll compare butterfly to the moths.

I need not no doctor nor medic nor shaman
To lift any stress or depression I feel
I just wander here to my bench by the lakeside
To see what no brushstrokes can ever reveal.

I come here each morning as dawn is approaching
Long before blackbird or robin or lark
To sit in an aura with muted companions
And watch the sunrise over Jilligoon Park.

J C Redmond

Untitled

Embrace each new day with the knowledge
That you can stand tall and know that you are loved.
Give in to your determination to make it through
And you will always find a way.
Look on the bright side.
Hold your head high and be at one with the world,
For you are.

L J Thomas

Dear Buttercup

Dear buttercup warm memories
Forever in your shine,
Gold ripples, laughter, whistled song,
Our thoughts that intertwine.

Dear buttercup soft healing peace
Enfolds me in your smile,
Re-read a chapter in our life
And stay with me awhile.

Jennifer Cox

My Prayer

Dear Lord don't let me dwell
On my aches and pains,
Or bore my friends with ancient tales,
Or fuss as I make my cups of tea
And discuss the price of my favourite cheese.
Let me laugh as I did in days gone by
Speak the best of folks tho' I have to lie,
Let me suppress the smile on my face
When quotes are made out of place,
And guard my tongue, when days are bad
As I wish for things I never had,
And as I wear my Sunday hat,
Don't let my head get too big for that.
Dear Lord if You hear this prayer
And discuss it with the saints up there,
One last request, the gift of mirth,
To hide all the tears I shed on Earth.

Phyllis Bowen

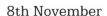

Kindness

Kindness is a gift
Kindness we can give to anyone
Kindness can be given any time
Kindness is today and always
Kindness is to be friendly
Kindness is an extended hand
Kindness is forgetting oneself
Kindness is a special happiness
Kindness spent in simply sharing
Kindness is to treasure the joys
Kindness is a happy smile
Kindness is loving words
Kindness that's above the rest
Kindness my love and gratitude
Kindness creates happiness
Kindness all the happiness it brings
Kindness is the simplest of things
Kindness that's important to you
Kindness be your guide
Kindness is a repayment
Kindness is quality time
Kindness is the power of love
Kindness is uplifting
Kindness not counting the cost
Kindness brings lots of love
Kindness in abundance
Kindness with joy and happiness
Kindness is to be blessed in every way
Kindness that God will richly bless.

Rita Scott

Daily Reflections

Forever In Our Hearts To Stay

Forever in our hearts to stay . . .
Is the love God gives today . . .
Though our way be winding and long . . .
His love is true, He gives a song . . .
Through all our nights, and all our days . . .
Forever in our hearts . . . He stays . . .

Carol Olson

House Of Forgotten Dreams

The trees and the garden are overgrown
The pool is full of stagnance and mud
Now as I stand in the house where I was born
I see every sunrise and every dawn.

It holds memories of tears and laughter
From the cellar to the cobwebbed rafters
From the dusty rooms I hear the silence
Charged with energy - and defiance.

The ghosts of the past don't give up easy
This house still hides so many secrets
The years have washed over this stately home
But from the shadows and gloom - a brightness glows

Now as a storm explodes from an angry sky
This big old house just creaks and sighs
I came here to lay all my demons to rest
I didn't think my heart would stand the test
And as I walk away it's so strange and it seems
I feel I've just stepped from a time machine
Just stepped from a time machine . . .

Frank Howarth-Hynes

God's Design

To certain conclusion, man must resign,
He can never equal God's design.
His mills grind exceeding slow.
First volcanic seeds he did sow,
Infinitely carefully raising
Chains of mountains and ranges of hills.

Then into newly-formed works
Wrought astounding great holes, for
With meteors Earth's crust he did bombard,
Creating greater and greater craters,
Before with one mighty blow,
He ripped matter clear,
Throwing it to clear space.

This molecular host slow, as it was no race,
Condensed and coagulated to
Set the moon in place.
Wild hot motion of this globe
Settled down, thus was created a world fated
Life to bring forth and nurture
Ensuring, enduring flora and fauna,
With man at its head, in God's image it has been said.

Man a privileged witness to results of snail-mills grinding,
As erosion of mountains and hills finding.
By violence built, gently but surely reduced to silt.
Filling large rivers, creating smooth plains,
Washed out to sea by thunderous, wondrous rains.
Earthquake and volcano will hasten the process,
From God's changing design,
There can be no divorces.

Graham Watkins

Laws Of Nature

Be it sound advice
For the best in life
Accept whate'er your day may bring
Even when thou feel a sting

Every little trial
Can bring some tranquil
Of something or another
To bring an onward spur

Seeking the laws of nature
Be an enduring future
When the way be found
Banishes all frown

Granted to everyone
Where'er they be under the sun
It is for thee to seek,
Whence thou doth reap

A new world awaits thee
Where'er thou be
Thy days be blessed
Life filled with zest

When following the laws of nature
Thy heart feels pure
The way of life sacred
And happiness thou spread

Giving time to pray
As thou travel thy way
Can release all sting
That the day may bring

Josephine Foreman

A Puddle

Head bent against the wind and rain
I trudge along the rutted path
On leaden, mud-caked feet.
The world around is grey and drear,
My thoughts echoing this gloomy landscape.
On cheerless winter days 'tis hard to realise
That this is but a passing phase
And bright times are just round the corner.

Then suddenly, my downcast eyes,
So used to viewing wind and rain,
Attracted are by lighter tones,
Not quite believing what I see -
A bright reflection in a puddle small
Held between the deep brown ruts,
A hint of blue, then blinding, golden flash
Reflected from above my head.
Slow to believe what I have seen,
I stop and raise my head.
The stinging rain has ceased to fall,
The wind has blown the clouds apart
And through the rift, the sun's bright rays
Gladden my heart, uplift my weary spirits:
New lease of life, fresh surge of hope,
The world around has changed -
And so have I!

Roma Davies

The Candle Of Christ

T ruth is all I have to give from within my once shallow heart,
H eaven by you to me has been shown without prejudice,
E very word, every sight to me by you, on to I have held,

C are is above all the most important feeling I have for you,
A dmiration for you I have every moment that together we spend,
N othing of your true beauty could ever be faulted,
D istance is that of being without you close by my side,
L ove is feelings that with a wretch like me you have blessed,
E ndless is our togetherness for all time and expansions,

O nly in an instance you shall take it if you desire my mortal heart,
F orgiveness and mercy upon my soul deeply scared did you to me show,

C hild of yours without shackles about me always have I been,
H orrendous I have been without any thought within my actions,
R evival I have been given with your spiritual breath,
I nnocence of none have I ever daily shown,
S pared yet you have, so that I may see your light,
T olerance have you always had, for this I am in your debt.

Shadow Duffield

Angels' Tears

Rain, rain, angels' precious tears,
Shed profusely to erase all our fears.

Gently received by Earth's eager embrace,
Absorbs and devours without a trace.

Passed on and delivered to all that desires,
Your comfort and strength lift us higher and higher.

Patricia Rose Thompson

Show You Care

If someone's sad and grieving
For a loved one who's not there,
Send a card or a few kind words
Just to show you care.

When a new member at your club
Stands, wondering what and where,
Don't turn away to talk to friends,
Go up and show you care.

If there's a friend or relative
With troubles they can't share,
Give a hug, a shoulder to cry on,
Tell them that you care.

This world of ours is full of strife,
Pain and hardships bring despair,
But we *can* make a difference
If we show we care.

Gwen Hoskins

Reflect On This

Just think how far the human race has come
since Neanderthal man rose from the swamp.
So many moons have waxed and waned. The pomp
and ceremony, trumpet-blast and drum
we blazon forth today were not perceived
by our first ancestors. They little thought
the lowly habitat for which they sought
would ever so outreach what they conceived.
They could not have imagined the recourse
to be within their wildest aspiration -
enough it was to wonder at creation -
to so much good and generous resource
God-given for the taking. His largesse
was lavished on His creatures. Their success

by slow degrees through ice and stone and iron
developed self-subsistence, self-respect,
to think their own invention could direct
their progress from primeval, tame the lion
couchant deep below ancestral skin.
The newly channelled dynamism went
to building steps allowing their ascent
to nobler aspirations than to win
some wild ephemeral prize through empty pride.
Despite the setbacks as they groped their way,
the snags, the hurdles, some manmade, yet they
evolved, as through a fire they'd been tried.
If only man today could cast his eyes
the way he'd come, he'd stand to his full size.

Adrian Brett

The Stranger

He was there at my birth,
my beginning,
He walked beside me
when a child, on life's road,
He was with me in youth's muddled confusion
when heavy a weight was my load.

I knew He was there in my loneliness,
I never felt Him when in temptation or wrong,
When my dam overflowed
He was with me,
He said
He'd been there 'all along'.

His presence was at my betrothal,
I felt Him so close in my fears,
I relied on His love so many times in my life
and He was there
in all the blessings and tears.

When I reached for the hand of
the stranger,
His hand was so firm and so strong,
I felt secure in my trust of
the stranger,
and sought Him, and believed, all life long.

He will be there at my death,
and my passing,
He will hold me,
my rock and my rod,
when
I shall touch the white hem of His garments
and look into the face of my God.

Diana Mudd

The Trees Grow Tall

*(A song written for the children of Carr-Bridge Primary School,
Inverness-shire who each planted a tree in the school grounds in 1998,
as the very last of them moved on to secondary school)*

The trees that we plant are our present
To those who will follow this way
A gift of goodwill for the future
The message of hope from today
We listen to past generations
In the stories we learn
Each day we are gaining the wisdom
That we should pass on in our turn

A new chapter starts
When the child is small
Then the world moves on
And the trees grow tall
As the sun shines down
And the raindrops fall
So the world moves on
And the trees grow tall
The magic of growth and renewal's
At risk if we fail to reflect
The Earth is a sensitive treasure
It's something we need to protect
It needn't be hard or expensive
If we all share the cost
From youngest to oldest amongst us
The stories must never be lost

A new chapter starts
When the child is small
Then the world moves on
And the trees grow tall

As the sun shines down
And the raindrops fall
So the world moves on
And the trees grow tall

David Gasking

The Time Of Life

Time was.
Time is.
Time will be.

The time of man
Is not the time of God.

Man's life on Earth lacks time.
Three score years and ten,
allotted span of beating heart.
Times of pleasure and of pain,
stress and strain and sorrow.
Rises up the constant cry,
'I must . . . I will . . . I need . . . I want . . .'
as if there's no tomorrow.
And the relentless rhythm
of the ruling clock
ticks away the present of man's life.

God's time is forever,
time and eternity
being the same.
Stop. Be still. Listen
to the measured beating
of the timeless clock
at the heart of the world.
See time present bridging
time which was and is to be.
And know that man will merge
with life eternal
in time. God's time.

Jean Bloomer

Curtain Call

At that lonely spot between cliff and moorland
On the high path
In the mist,
It was easy to believe I was being watched.
The billowing shrouds
Swirled like a flimsy ballet curtain
Barely concealing its excitation of waiting dancers.

A sigh from the coppiced-tree orchestra
And there the corps stood,
Silent tiptoe shadows.
Then I knew they were the audience:
I was on stage, the alien presence
Without even a tutu.

Only the mist stood between me
And the sixteen mystic does,
Standing motionless,
Their horned heads raised
In silent appraisal
Of an act none of them would applaud.

But, in a breath, they were gone
As noiselessly as they had arrived,
Disappearing
To some secret hedgerow hideaway
Where they could whisper
Secretly.

Oh that I could draw the magic mist
Around my shoulders
And vanish at will like the deer
Into my most private refuge.

Ted Harriott

Finding Freedom

I may not see clearly
But Jesus is here,
Right beside me.

With His help
I continue with the day.
Although I face many changes,
I need not be afraid.
For Jesus is with me,
Every step of the way.

For I choose to trust Jesus
To take care of me,
Knowing He loves me
Very much.

When I am in need
Of a helping hand,
Jesus is close by,
Giving me the help I need.

With Jesus by my side
I know I can make it,
Even though the journey may be tough.

For when I am weak
Then I am strong.
Strong in the Lord.
With His help nothing is impossible.

Julie Smith

Time To Dream

When angels spread their golden wings,
And mortal labours cease,
It is the time for dreaming,
Bold legends to release.

And as the moon goes cruising by,
A different world transcends.
A time of vivid fantasy,
Where truth is pleased to bend.

In this world of limbo state,
The heart can rule the mind.
All problems quickly vanish,
And weary souls unwind.

This dreamy mode transports you
To venues in your head,
Exploring far off kingdoms,
Your waking time won't tread.

For sleeping is a healer,
When snuggled in your bed.
Leave behind your heartaches,
And wander free instead.

Duchess Newman

He's My Everything

He's the crystal in every raindrop
that cascades from the skies.
He's the sapphire in the oceans and the seas.
He's the gold within the sunshine
that brightly shines above.
He's the emerald in the grass, the leaves and trees.

He's the diamond in the heavenly stars
studded in the night-time skies.
He's the ruby in the deepest, reddest rose.
He's the topaz in the cornfields
landscaped across the dales.
He's the beauty and the sparkle in our lives.

He's the gemstone in each flower bed
clustered in its fragrance sweet.
He's the precious stone that never ceases shining.
He's the opal in each heavenly cloud
that drifts within the skies.
He's the silver that's revealed within the lining.

He's the jewel within the rainbow
that glistens through the rain.
He's the amethyst that's used in works of art.
He's the Son of God called Jesus
who shed His precious blood.
He's the cultivated pearl within my heart.

What is money! What are values
when God's given us so much?
We are rich, so very rich, beyond all measure.
We've the finest master craftsman
to refine for us our lives.
Let Jesus be your priceless daily treasure.

Teressa Rhoden

A New Prayer

Dear Lord
Please hear my voice
I'm not asking for much
Just peace of mind
Allow me to love
And be loved back
Please make it soon
I'm asking You
I do have someone in mind
So my dear Lord
If you could be so kind
Sometime today
Please let her love
Become one with mine
I thank You Lord
And await a sign
Please let her love be mine.
Amen

Matthew Holloway

Have You Ever?

'Have you ever wondered about this place called Earth'?
Consider just a moment, about this thing called birth.
We do not know that we've been born until we're five or six,
We take everything for granted; I know that's what I did.
I believe it was when I was seven; I knew I was a person.
Then it was I asked my mum just how I came to be.
I was told not to ask questions, that really worried me,
Why had I to go to bed at night when I was wide awake
And get up every morning, and not sleep for sleeping sake.
One day my mother told me about the God up in the sky,
And all about Lord Jesus, His son with Him on high.
She taught me how to say my prayers before I went to sleep,
I had to be a good girl so good fortune I would reap.
Well I never found the fortune I didn't really care,
I was happy and contented to know he really cared.
Whenever I'm in trouble and things are not going right,
I give to God my burdens; ask Him to put them right.
My troubles I still have them, like everyone I know
Yet I recover quickly and never feel alone.
The fact that He is unseen, it seems to help me more
And wonder about Heaven, will there be an open door?
So I will carry on this journey and live as I think best
Until it's time to leave this Earth, and my worries put to rest.

Joan Prentice

My Beautiful Day

I borrowed a poem from the sky,
And music from a bird,
I stoke a chime out of the wind,
And from the rose a word.
I borrowed a song from the hills,
A psalm from the silver rain,
I took the footsteps of angels
Out of a cobbled lane,
From each little thing I fashioned
Something in my own way,
With God's help I put in my heart
A wonderful, beautiful day!

Marion Schoeberlein

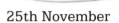

Verus Mendax

The woes for which all Heav'n sighs
The sins for which the Saviour died,
Chaste indulgence obedient ever at our side
The gospels' unrelenting pride;
In supplication we must go
With awe and reverence much in show,
Of mystery the host does sing
Such quietus does indoctrination bring;
With miracles blinding every eye
With platitudes hymn'd towards the sky,
The blessings of the bend'd knee
Absolve the soul so easily;
In the gift'd word we must rejoice
For veritas be the scriptures' voice,
Yet wherefore can free spirit be
When trite piety supplants philosophy?
With repentance as our very tithe
The mare of penitence shall we ride,
With devotion frenzied at the bit
Damnation cracks its patient whip;
Religion, that modernity and common-sense deride
And conviction holding both its sides,
That promise for which no evidence shows
Betrays the craft in faith we know.

M Sam Dixon

Who Are We?

England for the English
And Scotland for the Scots.
The Welsh have got their homeland.
And the Irish their shamrocks!

Now we are into Europe
Do we have to break in four?
Can't we still be British,
As we were in days of yore?

Pride seems to be old-fashioned.
We used to be so keen
On our United Kingdom
Reigned over by a Queen.

The British Isles is special,
It's been around so long.
Divided we are weakened -
Together we are strong.

Hurrah for devolution!
But do we need to break apart?
We could forget our differences -
We're all British - that's a start!

Lucy M Kaye

The Gift Of Words

The gift of words, a gift indeed
A way to communicate, that's what we need
A common language between all races
Whatever the colour of our faces
God's gifts of rain and wind and sun
Fall on each and every one
If God in His wisdom does not divide us
Why should mere men try to deprive us
Of life's greatest gifts?
Tho' not deserved
Of God's given blessing,
The gift of words.

Joan Winwood

Thank You, 'Lord'

Dear Lord in Heaven,
Let me take shelter,
Underneath an angel's wings,
Will You let me hear her,
As a beautiful song she sings?
Please Lord, let me rest a while,
Let me have time,
For just one more smile,
Let me feel the wind on my face.
Let there be no more pain,
As I leave this place,
Can I drink one last glass of wine?
Then let me go, for it is my time.
Thank You Lord,
My life was the best,
Now I gladly go with You
To take my rest.

Trudie Sullivan

I Try To Do Good

I try to do good
As I know that I should.
And I do what I do for the best.

Things don't always turn out
As I know without doubt.
But I really am trying my best.

Betty Mason

Leafy Lessons

Raindrops dripping down from forest trees
Fern and grasses bending in the strong breeze
And dark clouds in the sky hang low
Winding paths awash where travellers go

Birdsong hushed the only sound to hear
The pitter-patter of the raindrops far and near
No tiny creatures play beneath the trees
Nor yet the droning sound of busy bees

But now the rain has ceased the sun slants through
On the bracken raindrops shine in brightest hue
The mist has gone from mountain and from glen
The forest is transformed for us again

Woodland creatures join again in play
Enjoying now the freshness of the day
A robin washes in a sparkling pool
Its ruffled feathers skim the water cool

The scent of shady pines refreshed by rain
The bees around the foxgloves buzz again
Baby rabbits from their burrows come
To scamper in the grass warmed by the sun

These thoughts then we must take in context true
God has shown us what they mean for me and you
If He should send us sorrow, grief, or pain
He will always send us sunshine after rain

Doreen E Todd

Harvest Time

Glossy black, succulent and sweet,
In the hedgerows, nature's treat.
Blackberries abound - autumn's bounty,
On heath and moor, in every county.

We'll a-gathering go to harvest the berries
And guard our ankles with stout green wellies.
Our fingers and tongues with purple hue,
Show that we've sampled more than a few!

Chestnuts will follow, let the season unfold;
As the leaves turn from green to copper and gold.

Haden W Spicer

A Bedtime Prayer

30th November

Thank You Lord, for this beautiful day.
Thank You for the words I pray.
Help me Lord to understand,
And hold to Your unchanging hand.

Grant me peace as I rest this hour,
Guide me with Your holy power.
I pray that You will keep me safe,
From now on until daybreak.
Amen

Julliet Miller

Bittersweet

On this achingly beautiful spring day
my cry broke loose,
'Lord why should it be that today
my body is wracked with agonising pain?'
Then I remembered, on such a day as this,
the Lord of Life was slain.

Did the sparrows sing and fly
and rest upon Your tree,
did a turtle dove bill and coo;
was the emerging earth, for You
too bittersweet, the flowers too
glorious in their hue?

Would the offered spiked wine
have numbed Your senses then,
to re-creation and new birth;
when the die was cast,
and Your clothes changed hands,
before they sealed You in the earth?

And 'twas on such a morn as this,
that death was found to be a lie;
for You broke free from all
that would hold You down,
and rose triumphant over pain,
and by Your grace, Lord, so shall I.

Enid Riley

Starry Lullaby

The day is at a close . . .
My eyes are weary . . .
The dark sky, surrounding me,
Is starry . . .

I rest my little head . . .
Upon a nest of feathers . . .
My curtains draw, I close my door,
So starry . . .

Wearing my crinkled gown . . .
I soar away, away afar . . .
Into the moon, I nestle and swoon,
So starry . . .

I dream a mellow dream . . .
Of love and laughter and dancing . . .
The beautiful world, surrounding me,
Is starry.

Debbie Smith

Prayer To The Father

Father, I call on you
As now I think of those far-off days
Of my gentle father
His kindly ways
Gone, long years ago,
To his Heavenly rest
To You dear Lord
I make this request
Guide my prayer life
Let it grow
Binding me with those I know
Not just family and friends, but strangers too
Hear me Father when I call on You
Ever present, all my days
Bestow on me Your kindly gaze
My fears, my anxieties, joys I must
Bring to You in childlike trust
My earthly father's love I knew
Continues, magnified in You
May Your spirit guide me, this I ask
In performing every mundane task
And serving others' many needs
May silent prayer accompany deeds
Those unspoken words a blessing bring
That saddened hearts may laugh and sing
To our God with love and praise
The God of all our nights and days.

Brenda Hughes

The 'Me-Ness' In Me

(To my twin, Bill)

Leafing through all my snaps,
There seem to be umpteen mes.
You'd think I've changed perhaps
With many passing histories.

But no, within my very core
I have not grown a jot,
Looking back to days of yore
When I was just a tiny tot.

The lapse of years has much added
Experience to my credit
Even as the flesh has padded
With indulgence's strong habit.

Before birth's first painful breath
I had no identity.
When I succumb at last to death
I'll then erase the me in me.

Eileen Ellis-Whitfield

The Power Of Prayer

When doubts assail you, cling on to hope,
When troubles come and it's hard to cope,
You can reach God through the power of prayer,
He will hear you, He is always there.
Trust in Him to see you through,
He is with you in all you do.
He will give you comfort in your hour of need,
The power of faith is great indeed.
Talk to Him and share your fears
You can be sure that He always hears.
You have in God a faithful friend,
His strength and compassion to you He'll lend,
So be strong, have faith, to Him be true
And He in turn will be there for you.

Christine Naylor

The Lighthouse

There is but one lighthouse out in the sea,
one lighthouse which stands alone,
throughout the winter days and months
it guides the sailors home.
Colour is not of its making
for it looks so pure and white
and when the wind begins to moan
it sends out a hopeful light.
People rejoice in the tavern
and tell so many fine tales,
but only one lighthouse will guide them home
from wherever their boats have sailed.
Rocks and waves cannot harm them
for one lighthouse is there as a friend,
each sailor's thoughts and dreams unite
when the daylight quickly ends.
Far across the ocean wide
one lighthouse shines tonight,
bringing hope to all mankind
with soft and gentle light.
Storms will shake the mighty waves
as darkness fills the air,
but one tall lighthouse stands alone
with hope for all to share.

Tom Clarke

Sunrise

The fool has said within his heart
  that God does not exist,
that man evolved from nothing –
  creation is a myth!
But when I see the sunrise
dispel the morning mist –
I know that someone planned it:
I know that God exists!

He is a Master Artist
who paints the morning sky,
blends yellow, pink and orange
with grey and purple dye.
It changes every second
with ecstatic bursts of life,
'til darkened lifeless shadows
are lost in morning light!

Vera Smith

Maybe

Ifs, buts and maybes may seem the simple way out
but they discourage us from learning what life is all about.
Sometimes things can happen and we often wonder why,
it's hard to look for a rainbow in an overcast sky.
But life is made for what ifs as from these we learn,
mistakes make some sense when hope and faith take a turn.
Our being takes understanding the answers we may never know,
you can learn your potential if you're prepared to have a go.
You can't alter mistakes by moaning it doesn't get you anywhere,
looking on the dark side life seems gloomy and unfair.
If it all was so predictable how boring life would be,
mistakes are sent for a purpose in order to help you see.
If you are optimistic you can erase grey clouds of sorrow,
and look for the sunshine in the bright skies of tomorrow.

Lisa Thompson

Our God Is Able

When life is successful and happy,
and everything's going our way,
how easy to say God is gracious
and cares for the needs of each day.

When grey clouds are hiding the sunlight
and hopelessness makes us distraught,
how easy to question God's presence
and not give His blessings a thought.

But only when we are quite empty
can God teach the vital next step,
not working in anxious frustration
or trying to speed each thing up.

By patiently waiting upon Him,
we find the excess of His store,
be it wisdom or strength that is lacking,
He will give what we need and much more.

Diana Lynch

Uphill Struggle

When you have a mountain to climb,
You need all your strength all the time.
When the going gets tough, cling on,
Though the journey is very long.
Don't stop now, just keep on going,
In the end you will be growing.
To receive all the help you need,
Follow the path that seems to lead.

A Cooper

There You'll Go

They're honest, fair, they're kind, and true,
How much of this applies to you?
Do you confess, alone, at night,
To things you've done which weren't right?
Are you unfair, in verbal strife,
To children, friends, or man, or wife?
The power of intellectual might
Should not be used to prove you're right.
Intelligence brings no reward
To those who wield it like a sword,
While truthful, humble things we've said
Will be remembered when we're dead.
If you say things which cause offence,
I'm only human's no defence,
Don't ever be the cause of woe,
If there's a Heaven, there you'll go.

Matthew L Burns

. . . Trust In God . . .

My God, You have created me to do You some definite service,
You have given some definite work to me which You have given no other.
I know that I have my place in Your vast and wondrous plan;
I may never know exactly what it is in this life,
but I know You, my God, will let me know what it is
in the next life, in Heaven.

Therefore I will trust You in all things.

If I am sick, may my sickness serve You.
If I am in sorrow, may my sadness serve You.
If I am worried, may my worry serve You.
If I am in pain, may my pain serve You.
If I am alone, may my loneliness serve You.

You do nothing in vain; You know what You are doing.
You may take away my family; You may put me among strangers;
You may make me feel forgotten; You may make my spirit sink;
You may hide my future from me; You may make my life feel empty;
Yet still You know what You are doing and I trust You dear God in all things.
May all have trust in You dear God, like I do.

Sophie Anne Storey

My Work Lord

The Lord works in mysterious ways
His wonders to perform.

Wherever He places me today
I will do my best to conform.

I am a child of God
A channel of His peace,
I ask in humble grace,
Here I am Lord, send me.

Susan Haldenby

Watching

How lovely it is, to listen
To the wings of the morning
And be still in the dawn
When turning to the day.
A practical peace arises,
Its presence to guide you,
Accompany you, and extend
The hand of courage for
Whatever is to be faced.

How beautiful to know
That all is well underneath
The hours of dark and light.
To feel enveloped
By the ineffable that is
Beyond your little self.

How comforting to dwell daily
With secret silence holding you
In safety with each step.

How restful to sink nightly into
The sacred sleep of sunset.

How wonderful it is to watch.

Judith Thomas

Tenby Winter Moonlight

The crisp moon, shining on the snow
Set our small town aglow
Giving back into the night
An equal shining light

The tips of the waves
As they gently swept the caves
Carried jewels bright
On this cold winter's night

The moonlight, its beauty to unfold
Turned the sea into a sheet of gold
And with its magician's hand
Caressed the soft ochre sand

Gifts from God we bring
To this small town
Dressed overall in your white gown
Gifts fit for a king

The majestic cliffs, with crowns of white
Stood in homage at this sight
Proud, dark and strong
Guarding their domain, ere long

Avis Nixon

Waiting

Waiting - what for?
Waiting in the quiet of the night for the dawn,
when the light of the sun, like God's love
creeps above the horizon,
playing on the moving sea, shining on the sand,
spreading across the world,
illuminating our lives, an integral part of life's force.

Waiting in our hearts once more
for the coming of God's son.
Love in a manger,
the strength and vulnerability of the world,
worshipped by the unlikely,
celebrated by millions, but not yet known by some.

Waiting - what for?
- For the dark empty spaces in our lives to be transformed yet again?
- For the hope and peace of the world to be rekindled?
So let us wait, like excited children
for the celebration of God's precious gift.
Let us wait with patience
and then make way for the light of the world,
for the light of Christmas.

Ann Brown

Christmas Love

The days to Christmas fall like autumn leaves,
White squads of cards swell in the postman's bag
And Christmas envelopes snowflake the floor
Where quick excited fingers pick them up.
The young man gathers up his clutch of cards
And takes them to his haven in the study.
He ekes out the slow-motion discovering of identity.
He scans the writing, looks at the postmark,
Notes the stamp, opens the envelope, takes out the card.
Someone has thought, someone has cared,
Not always indeed with complete sincerity,
Yet it is best to credit the writer
With goodwill, kindness, care and love
Than toss the card aside with cynicism.
Each card he handles with a lingering touch
And makes himself receptive to the messages:
Best wishes, greetings, love.
He makes much of love.
No sign of love is to be wasted
And in receiving it with reverent hands
The love is multiplied.

The youthful priest in silence goes about his work
So slowly and unhurried.
He treads the sanctuary with careful feet
Rapt in a confident fragility,
Repeating the oft-repeated
With awe, humility and gratitude
Holding awhile those tokens of His passion.
The Bread and Wine are merging into focus,
A sign and symbol of a steady love.

Howard Sainsbury

Daily Reflections

Friendship Candle

(In memory of Mary Williams - author -
a talented, kind and sincere friend)

Light two little candles, give one to a friend.
From such small beginnings, grows a chain that cannot end.

Just one little candle, can light so many more,
Spreading the light of friendship, to all earth's distant shores.

Just one little candle, can brighten up each day,
Guiding men to Jesus; He is the Light, the Truth, the way.

So even when the night is dark, you still can see a light.
Then you'll know that friendship candle is forever burning bright.

Mary Williams

Moment In Thought

(Dedicated to David)

When someone goes from the sight of your eyes,
They draw much closer to the beat of your heart
Like a starless sky on a midsummer night
They linger there, just out of sight
Wrapped within one's memory
Just as sure as night follows day
Everything in life has a part to play
Even the past is just one thought away.

Mary Veronica Ciarella Murray

Open Immediately – Gift Enclosed

Thank God for what the angels sang
Two thousand years ago –
A song that round the heavens rang
And on the earth below –

About a gift to save mankind
From sin for evermore,
Wrapped up by God and pers'n'ly signed,
Delivered to our door.

No junk mail this, no catalogue,
No bill, but real free gift;
Enough to set your eyes agog
And give your heart a lift.

There is no closing date to beat,
Condition to be met,
Small print that will your eyes defeat –
Just payment of sin's debt.

So write your thank you letter quick
And send it back above;
It's postage paid, no stamp to stick.
Then live in heav'nly love.

David Varley

A Candle Burning

We don't need no fancy Christmas lights
coloured other than white
no fancy ribbons and flashing neon lights
only a candle, one solitary guiding light

for we have all we need, Lord
in the faith and love we share
with You and all others who care
a solitary flame is enough to see us through

to remember of the day he came
wrapped in swaddling clothes he lay
while outside and all around
elders and learned, knelt and prayed

nor do we need to look far for Your love
it is in everything we see
the trees, butterflies, birds and bees
the glowing sun, spring rain and winter snow

for we have all we need
bestowed on us every day
such Your love that You freely give
of no greater gift can we hope to learn

than be like You, as to others we give
for whether it be day or night
Your candle burns in our hearts
Your light showing us the way

the solitary flame of the candle
being a symbol of Your love
that is why we need no coloured Christmas lights
for daily, we are showered with Your undying love.

Maurice Hope

The Ultimate You!

The 'sun'-ny disposition of Your smile beamed around the Earth;
The 'sky'-blue tears reigning down from Your eyes;
The trees swaying in the wind - Your daily wave of 'hello';
The dawn chorus of birdsong.

The gentle caress of Your kiss carried by the breeze on
                                    a warm summer's night;
The greatest artist of all - Creator of all wonders and
                                    natural landscapes;
The night sky - reflections of Your 'light' in my soul;
The eternal 'dreamcatcher'.

The 'still small voice' crying out in the desert of mankind;
The cascading waterfalls, reminders of the passage of time
                                    and the rejuvenation of the spirit;
The warm radiance of Your being wrapped up in mine
The 'protector' and Saviour during my darkest moments.

God - the ultimate You!

Lisa S Marzi

One Beautiful Morning

The weak winter sun shines bleakly
Throughout the silver sky
The little robin sings meekly
Reaching the notes so high.

Oh what a beautiful morning
Snowflakes, like gold dust, falling to the ground
The men are looking for logs to bring
To start a fire for us to sit around

I see children throwing snowballs
Striving to keep warm
Their faces are like little dolls
Enjoying the fun before being caught in the next snowstorm.

This is my ideal window scene
It'll soon be Christmas day
The children can't wait; they're ever so keen
With each one of them showing it in their own special way!

Louise Pamela Webster

Christmas (Peace At Last)

The house is silent;
Outside, snow settles
Like dandruff.
The house is silent;
Inside, lights, owl-like,
Blink to greet the dawn.
The house is silent;
Save for echoes of family squabbles
And tales of tragedy.
The house is silent.

Rad Thomas

There's Always A Rainbow

There's always a rainbow,
Though sometimes it hides,
Clouded by sorrow,
Blown away by our sighs.

The hope and the joy
Buried deep in our heart
Need some space to emerge,
And then we can start
To see the bright colours
That light up our path.

When you can't see the rainbow,
Just be still, and ask.

Erica Wishart

Christmas Time

It is Christmas time.
I love the excitement.
That sense of anticipation
which enchants me.

I become a child again!
In wonder I gaze
at the twinkling lights
like stars in the sky.

Shops all decked out,
colour and sparkle abound
with presents gaily wrapped
and ribbons and bows galore.

How diligently I search
for that special little gift
that will surprise
and delight and bring joy.

The fairy on the Christmas tree
has such a commanding view
of her tree all decked out
and happy family smiles and fun.

Light bulbs, red, green, blue and yellow
accentuate each decoration and gift
and send a glow of warmth
to all the passers-by.

Carols fill the air
and there is music
in the hearts of young and old
reflecting the love that came
with that birth so long ago.

Pamela Gillies

Come – Let Us Adore Him

In wintertime,
Bright log fires give out a 'warm' glow
grey-leaden skies
dissolve, into light flaky snow.
The earth so hard
hugs the snow, as it softly falls,
by morning
mirrored ice, flanked by snowy walls.

Children play
their shouts of delight, fill the air
Snowmen appear!
Bleak, naked trees, holly, bright berries bear.
Bright afternoon sun
crisp air, then suddenly! Biting wind and sleet,
darkness falls early
homeward-bound children, cold hands, wet feet.

Parents call out
Come, see the tree, pretty with presents and glitter.
It's almost Christmas!
Come, and be warm, forget the wind - so bitter.
Let us remember
Jesus the King who was born on this Earth,
Let's celebrate!
He came as our Saviour, and died, to give us . . .
                    New birth!

Beryl Lenihan

Friends Forever

When it seems the whole world
Has come to an end there is always
A person remaining with you
Who is a true companion.

He that shares your pains
And feels your sorrows
He that rejoices with you
On the day of happiness

A true friend will remain faithful
To you in all situations whenever
You look back he's always there
Ready to assist when your strength is failing

Joys and pains you've shared together
These are worlds that you've built
Around yourselves that make you strong
And face the stress of friendship forever

Memories of good and bad times
You've had together become the
Bonds that keep you going in
Time of trials.

A true friend is scarce to get
But having him around is so
Fulfilling and full of fun
That truly reveals a lasting love.

A true friend will make you not to
Worry about life because, whenever
You turn around you find him around
When you're down, he shows he cares

A friend in need is a friend in deed
A true friend that is always forever.

Adegoke Austin Adedamola

When Love Came Down At Christmas

When Love came down at Christmas
In the form of a baby boy
No one could envisage
That He would bring such joy.

For Love heals all sorrow
Love unites each other
As Jesus taught us how to pray
For one another.

'Love came down at Christmas'
Rossetti wrote one day
Her carol reminds us daily
That Jesus is here to stay.

Marian Bythell

The Peace Of God

Just a short distance from our home
we can walk alongside a very beautiful stretch of waterway.
At quite short distances apart, small red-brick bridges span the water. Their reflec-
tions in the water are sharply defined.
Everything speaks of the peace of God.
The lush vegetation each side of the waterway,
with its myriad of insects pollinating the seasonal flowers,
is a delight and balm to the senses. As you stroll along
the peace and beauty enfolds you like the love of God.

The waterway has a constant, gentle movement
as the stately swans, ducks and other native waterfowl,
glide back and forth their chosen territory.
The water reflects the colours around and glistens and sparkles.
Such beauty, such peace.

One is reminded of the words,
'When peace like a river floods into the soul.'
When the peace of God enters our souls
there are no words adequate to describe it.
The canal walks are a constant and lovely reminder of this gift of peace.

On a crisp and snowy Boxing Day at the end of last year,
a colourfully decorated longboat was breaking a way through the ice
for the vulnerable waterfowl to get to clear water.
As we waved a greeting to the two men steering the boat
we noticed the name of the boat was *Shalom.*
How fitting a name indeed.
Peace can so often thaw the iciest of hearts;
God's peace that passeth understanding.

Thelma Robinson

Tired Eyes

I'll paint you a rainbow
Through dark clouds
Float you a kiss on the breeze
Portray your face in each raindrop
Whisper my love through the trees
Send you a bouquet of sunsets
With love wrapped in summer blue skies
Pluck beautiful diamonds
From the dewdrops
With sparkle to match your blue eyes.
We'll paint us an end to our rainbow
Empty the crock of its gold
Fill it with love for a lifetime
And cherish it as we grow old.
As time maps our face
With life's troubles
And years streak the silver
To our hair
Tired eyes fade the colours
Of our rainbow
We'll have beautiful memories
To share.

B Wardle

The Best Day Of My Soul

Whene'er I lay the pillow
And dream the day gone by
I ponder should it be my last
Then this prayer I sigh
'Lord I am that sinner
You said you would give rest
Now death has come to try my trust
And put it to the test
For Lord I am that prodigal
Who turned to search Your face!
When death did come and stripped from me
All I own . . . but Faith!'

Yet should I rise my pillow
And think the day arrived
I pray my Lord will find my soul
More pleasing to His eyes
That I should strive to find His love
In everything I see
In all of His creation made
That is His gift to me
Until that day I fall to sleep
On a pillow hewn from stone
For God to smile He beckoned me
On the best day of my soul!

M J Banasko

For Peace

Peace lies ahead, though dim as yet its light.
Testing and anxious though the journey be
Doubt not, my heart, the outcome of the fight.
At times it seems we toil through darkest night;
Yet struggle on, at last you shall be free;
Peace lies ahead, though dim as yet its light.
Many before us knew the self-same plight,
By their example guiding you and me.
Doubt not, my heart, the outcome of the fight.
If disbelief seems strong, if faith seems slight,
Again at break of day our path we see.
Peace lies ahead, though dim as yet its light.
Honour the brave who hold our wavering sight,
Whose words and deeds in all respects agree.
Doubt not, my heart, the outcome of the fight.
So let not fear or anger cast their blight.
Our Lord leads on to all eternity.
Peace lies ahead, though dim as yet its light,
Doubt not, my heart, the outcome of the fight.

Kathleen M Hatton

Patience In Life

I can give you life so that you may enjoy all things,
In your life I will give you my blessings.
Mark these words in stone to remind,
Use these as milestones in your life, your way to find.
Tread this path of faith then life will be true,
Ponder not as you travel, look into horizon's sky of blue.

Tribulation will tap you on the shoulder,
But patience is earned and it makes you bolder.
Earn you this gift through faith and prayer,
Listen to my voice in your heart as you travel far.
Heed my advice then what befalls you,
Then remember my friendship is the one that's true.

Take this life I give you, hold it in your heart, firmly,
Then true love will be with you and your family.
Be patient with the children in your care,
I gave them life, like you, cherish it and share.
Heed my philosophy, walk straight and do not stray,
Then happiness will be with you forever and a day.

John Clarke

Thanks

How can I say thanks for being there?
How can I show that I really care?
A friend like you is so hard to find.
Your fun, you're great, helpful and kind.

How can I say thanks for your shoulder I cry on?
For the hours of talk till the pain is all gone.
You're my strength, my laughter, I love you so much.
You understand things that others can't touch.

How can I say thanks for a friendship that lasts?
Through the ups and the downs we've had in the past.
For all that we've gone through, the thick and the thin.
Forever, without you, where would I begin?

Thanks to you for being my friend.
And friends we will stay right through to the end.
It's friendship that grows with each passing day
But before I go I've got something to say . . .

> *Thanks*
> *I love you x*

Sally Mather

Time And Us

Time places its
Mark upon us,
It makes us
Grow old,
It makes us
Grow strong,
It makes us
Who we are.

Christina Earl

Come Hither, New Year

(To my very dearest mother, Mrs Merna Crossley,
with very much love and affection from her elder son, Michael!'

- So with such magical momentum
Flying into our lives in an
Ever-speeding way –

- There is constant motivation
For our own sustainable usefulness
To serve both the
Gladness and the sorrow together.

- Then mightily moving over us
With all of our deepest suppressions.
As they each gather some
Fervently emotional delight to
Enrapture the fibres and souls of our
Very being for evermore –

Now that we each live in the present,
Hereby graciously glancing backwards
And forwards to the
Persistently explosive minefields of daily life.

- So come hither, new year.

Michael Denholme Hortus Stalker

Daily Reflections
2005
A to Z of Authors

A to Z of Authors

461

Information

We hope you have enjoyed reading this book - and that you
will continue to enjoy it in the coming years.
If you like reading and writing poetry drop us a line, or give us
a call, and we'll send you a free information pack.

Write to:
Triumph House Information
Remus House
Woodston
Peterborough
PE2 9JX
Tel: 01733 898102
Email: info@forwardpress.co.uk